A Bibliography
of Conceptual Writing

A Bibliography
of Conceptual Writing

v1.01

compiled by
yigru zeltil

khora impex // 2017

cover based on: derek beaulieu, extract from *The Duchamp Opening* (2016-05-29); Calgary. No press.

ISBN: 978-1-365-72551-7.

http://khora-impex.com/

The business of a poet [...] is to examine, not the individual, but the species; to remark general properties and large appearances: he does not number the streaks of the tulip, or describe the different shades in the verdure of the forest.

(Samuel Johnson, *The History of Rasselas, Prince of Abissinia*, chapter 10, paragraph 6.)

(Jorge Luis Borges, *El Idioma Analítico de John Wilkins*[1])

---

[1] Pablo Katchadjian vs. María Kodama.

note

This project consists of a permanent work-in-progress chronological list (that will continue to be updated and is accessible at http://workinprogressconpo.blogspot.com/2016/08/the-bibliography.html) and a bibliography of a somewhat more traditional format (authors sorted alphabetically, books sorted chronologically), that is now published with the launch of my own platform, 'khora impex' (co-founded with Sebastian Big, whose books I also had to include here), and may eventually receive a massively revised second edition of my own, but is going to remain open source – in other words, feel free to make your own, hopefully better edition.

This edition is meant to provide stable reference, as a Blogger page or even any other kind of Web page may never be as safe as a printed format. Even before publishing this edition, I was informed by one author of their intention to create an entire library of conceptualism. In spite of many of these books being digital and/or print-on-demand or simply (nearly) impossible to obtain (anymore), it can indeed serve also as a 'shopping list'. Aside being a consumption or collectors' aid, my bibliography is meant as a resource for people who are passionate about the phenomenon and scholars alike (though most authors, critics, readers come from the academia).

As of now, it includes than 1,100 digital and print volumes (from chapbooks to anthologies and even a few books on the topic of conceptual writing) and magazine issues (for example, *0 TO 9* is collected in its entirety in the 2006 book credited to Acconci and Mayer, so I haven't made other entries for it). (**Warning:** book titles are in full and uncensored!)

The cataloging was done using search engines, book databases, anthologies such as *Against Expression* and *I'll Drown My Book*, articles, publishing house pages and so on – just on-line resources (with few exceptions), since I do not have access to libraries overseas or the ability to order a significant amount of books just for this purpose. (Which is why I allow you, if you are more knowledgeable than me, to pick up this bibliography and add what is missing or change format, unless you only wish to contact me and merely suggest additions.) Having to recheck everything as I completed this edition, I made so many inquiries in a short period of time that, more than once, I was forced to prove I am not a robot…

It turned out necessary for me sometimes to trust in blurbs or references in other books, as an excerpt is not available, especially if the book still seems 'conceptual enough'. For this reason, certain books may be removed in the future as it will become possible for me to check them. However, I am fairly certain that most, if not all, of these books (and magazines) may partially or entirely be described as 'conceptual' (as long as we do not confine its meaning to austere uses of appropriation, read more on my opinion the foreword below); in a few cases, it may be just one relevant text (that is the case with the Hart Crane anthology, to give an example that is also present in *Against Expression*).

There are some cases in which the selected authors may have more eligible books than are cataloged here and others in which authors present in anthologies or magazines may not otherwise be present with their individual (and eligible) books. Furthermore, there may still be books which I could have discovered and cataloged while, for instance, browsing the series of their publishing houses, while some books were inevitably off my radar because of belonging to China, Iran, Russia and other spaces about which it proved very hard for me to find more information.

Then there are probably many books of experimental[2] literature that may be considered borderline examples of conceptualism (or aren't so borderline, but I could not figure if they should really be considered 'conceptual writing' instead of merely concepts of conceptual artworks or performances, like in the case of Yoko Ono's *Grapefruit*, not to mention all the artist books that are rather classified as sculptures; I've made an exception for Morten Søndergaard's box set of objects *Ordapotek* (*Wordpharmacy*), as the textual component is essential and as it was registered with ISBN), books which are classified in virtue of being important 'proto-conceptual' examples (the assumption being that Diderot or Mallarmé more essential in this matter than Cervantes,

---

[2] As broad/vague as it may seem, I prefer this term to, say, 'avant-garde'. As the Tirana-based publishing house named *Uitgeverij* (meaning 'publisher') say, we do not like the word 'avant-garde'; we are not in the military (http://www.uitgeverij.cc/about/).

Sterne, Flaubert or Lautréamont – yet these are situations detailed or at least mentioned in the few theory books also cataloged here), as well as cases in which I had to not include something that may be meant as a conceptual artist book/literary work, but seems to be just a piece of non-fictional writing that serves its own purpose – a 'real thing', not its appropriation (and vice versa, I may have included by accident a few such books that seemed to function as conceptualist).

That at least some conceptual books may be confused by some readers with the 'real thing' (not unlike what happened in the context of minimal art) is a different and equally funny story… I tried my best to single out, for instance, examples of concrete poetry that can be accurately enough considered conceptual as well – Pedro Xisto's *a e i o u* (1966) is such a fine example, some of Aram Saroyan's minimal poems also fit here –, but I may have classified as 'conceptual writing' some works that have more to do with 'visual arts' and less with writing in itself. At least for now, I'm going to leave these borderline examples alone (some of them already classified by others as 'conceptual writing', mind you), as they could be of interest to those who study all this anyway – no big deal and I am certainly not pretending that I have managed to make a flawless job. This is a bibliography that may at any time become more rigorous – no problem…

P.S. There are a couple of recent books that are notably missing from this catalog – *FLARF: An Anthology of Flarf* (edited by Drew Gardner, Gary Sullivan, K. Silem Mohammad, Nada Gordon and Sharon Mesmer, Edge Books), which should have come out on 2016-12-19 (according to the data on Google Books), but was not confirmed to me by the poets themselves, and *Crude Love. Essays on Post-Conceptualism* (edited by Kim Rosenfield and Steven Zultanski), which was due for the same month and already had an ISBN as well, but was deleted from the Ugly Duckling Presse site as of now (Matvei Yankelevich let me know that it may still come out, but 'not very soon'). The same publishing house also has a few other interesting forthcoming titles (Mónica de la Torre's *The Happy End / All Welcome*), but I'd prefer now to catalog them in the next edition, after they have been released for sure. You can keep your eyes peeled on the blog in the meantime…

Edit (2017-02-01): Because of the technical issues around the file that I uploaded on Lulu, I was forced to change the formatting and comply with this boring template. There is no big difference between this edition (that I decided to name v1.01) and what the first five people who bought it without problems got, aside just some newer additions (such as Carlos Almonte and Alan Meller or Richard Prince) and a few minor revisions in the foreword (added below a footnote mentioning a Craig Dworkin book on 'blank' books), as well as optimizing the book for black and white printing.

for/word

I don't think, nor do I think anyone should think, intertextuality, erasure, pastiche, performance, docupoetics, neobaroque poetics, ecopoetics, ethnopoetics, experimental lyricism, and so on, are practices that need to be included explicitly under the banner of "Conceptual poetry." At best, Conceptual poetry is just one practice amid these other practices, and that's fine, and that shouldn't even be the center of our concerns because there are structures of exclusion that are much more insidious, of much greater import, than the mode or style a text was made in. (Aaron Apps, *An affective response*[3])

It started out as just a Goodreads list in which I bunched together volumes excerpted/mentioned in *Against Expression: An Anthology of Conceptual Writing* and a few other books that I stumbled upon and thought of as 'conceptual' (it just seems irresistible to use, even though I also enjoy encountering authors and/or books that can't really fit in boxes).

This was in part due to the ridiculous limitations of Goodreads, site which has a kind of genre or tagging system, but does not let users browse through all the books of one such category (or even other categories such as by publishing house or collections). Then the list itself turned out to be too limited

---

[3] http://jacket2.org/article/affective-response

and I didn't want to game the system (making multiple accounts just so I can exceed the vote limit), so I abandoned it for a while until the idea of an old-fashioned bibliography emerged (in I still can't remember what circumstances).

It turned out that not even Kenneth Goldsmith tried to build a more or less 'global' bibliography of conceptualism, as he told me in private when mentioning my idea. *Notes on Conceptualisms* (Fitterman/Place), *Against Expression...* (Dworkin/Goldsmith) and *I'll Drown My Book: Conceptual Writing by Women* (Bergvall/Browne/Carmody/Place) may (at least in part) function as such; I also thought at first that Dworkin's *The Perverse Library* could be what I am looking for. It did generate at the time an exhibition of 'conceptual writing' that was conceived by Simon Morris, who made for this occasion a so-called *Bibliography of Ugly Cousins*, consisting in 'critical examples of appropriated writing, or 'rip-offs', that expose the parasitic relationship between conceptual writing / writers and their histories.'[4] Still, nothing exactly like what I was about to start.

Since I was educated in the spirit of sincerity rather than cynicism, I should be open about my reasons for carrying out such a project, so here it goes... Aside my honest pleasure for making lists (and for the subject itself[5]), it could be said that this is an

---

[4] http://www.informationasmaterial.org/portfolio/the-perverse-library-exhibition/

[5] As Darren Wershler puts it in one of his articles (http://www.alienated.net/academic-writing/conceptual-writing-fanfic/), conceptual writing can be seen as a

excuse for me to network with the authors I am
going to translate or attract some attention
for my own poetic projects (most of them due
to be released in the near or distant future)
and I'm not denying it – being yet another
Romanian poet trying to get away, at least for
a while, from the conservative culture…

(While indeed echoing the name of Tristan
Tzara (*trist în ţară*/'sad in the/my country')
and the upstart urge of Isidore Isou, I try
not to make grand claims of un/originality,
even if I naturally reached by myself certain
conceptual procedures by reacting against what
the Romanian writers from the generation
before me imposed: the autobiographical, the
visceral – modes which implied a certain brute
notion of authenticity, an equivalence between
writing and living (a Beat kind of living). My
life, on the other hand, tends to be
inadequate for narrative description; more
than actions or even people, I see the areas
of data, of information, systems, colors,
patterns and modular dreams – things which do
cause me emotional associations, nothing truly
'indifferent'. So from early on it felt
inadequate for me to write about them, but
only after I discovered the possibility of
working directly within their frames – like
bringing together my favorite entries from a
dictionary I grew up with or from the Yellow
Pages.)

As an outsider, I am aware of my advantage –
I'm not one of 'those' conceptualists that
have already done so many things to 'control'

---

kind of 'fanfiction' (or, as I might add, a low-budget
version in some cases) of conceptual art, so you too may
perceive this as such – count me in.

the 'brand' of conceptual writing that some, as I've heard especially after *The Body of Michael Brown*, have tried to get away from the label, as it has been indeed tainted (nevertheless, conceptualism is still productive, even if it will step out of the spotlight). All I can do is acknowledge this real issue of racist intents and political incorrectness and make with this bibliography the following point…

Whether it is purely formalist in intent, with poetic undertones (like in some texts from I'll Drown My Book: Conceptual Writing by Women) or taking more or less a political stance (aside classic examples of détournement, we could invoke here Madeline Gins' *What The President Will Say and Do!!* from 1984, Emmett Williams' anti-war concrete poem *SOLDIER* – included in the 1973 volume *A Valentine for Noël* and recently reissued as a standalone book –, Sergio Pesutic's *La hinteligencia militar* – the only blank-page[6] book I have included here, as its subversive title made the authorities in Chile ban it – or M. NourbeSe Philip's *Zong!*), conceptual practices have been, are and will be practiced around the world – of course, as long as certain conditions make it possible and desirable (unable to expand here, but there have to be writing necessities that can't be fulfilled by regular conventions).

Sure, conceptualism as a distinct movement seems indeed largely confined to not so many countries: from Canada and the USA (in which even the notion of conceptual writing as

---

[6] See Craig Dworkin's *No Medium* (2013, The MIT Press) for more on this topic.

analogon to conceptual art may date back to the days of the L=A=N=G=U=A=G=E group; as for Moscow Conceptualists, I don't know enough to give an opinion on whether Marjorie Perloff is right or not in her point of view[7]) to Scandinavia or the UK; as for France, there have been things like Éditions Lorem Ipsum or Éditions de l'Attente, earlier or current book artists like Claude Closky, F. Dumond or Bernar Venet, but the 'dots' seem to be not so connected... Still, the map that can be made out of this bibliography would show enough other – smaller, it's true – spots, all the way from Chile to the Philippines. If/when things are going to get even more 'global' is not up to me, as disseminating information is not enough. It takes belonging to a certain set of sensibilities and being already open-minded and (un?)creative enough to pick up such practices, especially where it is not already encouraged and institutionalized (which allows one to be more independent... and safe from the criticism of having hijacked the symbolic value of poetry! Even Craig Dworkin suggested thinking of conceptualism as an unified spectrum of practices across disciplines...).

As for the quote from Aaron Apps... I did took the liberty of including here several of those practices in my scope. Why not? Conceptual writing, as it has been defined so far in North America, cannot be reduced to appropriation. As Laynie Browne and Caroline Bergvall have argued already in the intros to *I'll Drown My Book: Conceptual Writing by Women*, conceptualism can and should be defined in a more inclusive manner. (While loose – in

[7] https://lareviewofbooks.org/article/the-gray-area-an-open-letter-to-marjorie-perloff/

itself, it looks like it may describe a lot of different 'postmodern' strands -, the classification provided in the anthology does offer more clues on the wider field of conceptualism: *process (constraint, mimicry, mediation, translative, versioning), structure (appropriation, erasure, constraint, formula, pattern, palimpsest), matter (baroque, hybrid, generative, corporeal, dissensual) and event (documenta, investigative, intertextual, historicism, speculative).*)

One idea I insist mentioning here is that of Peli Grietzer from the article *The Aesthetics of Sufficiency: On Conceptual Writing*[8]: that, inhabiting a kind of 'negative space of ordinary literature', conceptual writing can still provide writers and readers alike fresh outlooks beyond the hackneyed, been-there-readymade-done-that aspects, at least if we pay attention to the 'semi-creative' writers out there who are not necessarily 'against expression', lyrical poetry, identity politics or other things... As another author (I can't seem to find the article right now for some reason) suggested, it's not that hard to get into conceptualism, as it is (for some, too) transparent – though rarely as literally predictable as some of the works of Todd Van Buskirk, which announce you the whole content and structure of the book from the cover, the same phrases that are used as title being repeated throughout the rest of the pages... (The print-on-demand platforms are full of other such 'monster' books, another example being Holly Melgard's *BLACK FRIDAY* with its 740 pages of black ink on white paper,

---

[8] https://lareviewofbooks.org/article/the-aesthetics-of-sufficiency-on-conceptual-writing/

foregrounding the technical issues around Lulu's printing services.)

I have to stop here, as I did not really plan to write here a grand essay on all these matters (leaving it for another occasion). Just wanted to clarify a few things before deploying the enormous list... OK, if you want more about conceptualism and, eventually, revised editions of this bibliography, just keep an eye out on the 'khora impex' page in the following years. As for feedback, you may find me on social media or just send me a mail on yigruzeltil@yahoo.com. For now, credit goes to derek beaulieu, Angela Genusa (who helped me a lot with this revision), Kenneth Goldsmith, Joseph Mosconi, Matvei Yankelevich, Joey Yearous-Algozin and others I may have forgot to mention, all contributing in direct and indirect ways.

yigru zeltil // 2016-2017

___ (1999). *OEI #1 - Oidentifierade verbala objekt*. Stockholm.

___ (2000). *Action Poétique n°158, « Poésie (&) Ready-Made »*. Paris: Farrago/Les Belles Lettres.

___ (2000). *OEI #4-5 - KRTK*. Stockholm.

___ (2001). *OEI #7-8 - EFTER LANGUAGE [samtida innovativ amerikansk poesi]*. Stockholm.

___ (2002). *OEI #9-10 - Alla talarr svännska*. Stockholm.

___ (2003). *OEI #14 - GERTRUD ST(O)EIN*. Stockholm.

___ (2003). *OEI #15-17 - Appropriering*. Stockholm.

___ (2004). *OEI #18-21 - Textkonst*. Stockholm.

___ (2004). *OEI #22-23 - ELEKTROEI*. Stockholm.

___ (2006). *OEI #27 - suOmEI*. Stockholm.

___ (2007). *OEI #31-32 - r's (un)digest*. Stockholm.

___ (2007). *OEI #33-35 - NONSENS*. Stockholm.

___ (2008). *OEI #37-38 - (R)ed*. Est. Stockholm.

___ (2008). *OEI #39-41 - Mix-Up!*. Stockholm.

___   (2008-07-29). *Tidsskriftet 28/6*.
København: Forlaget 28/6.

___   (2009). *OEI #43-45 - biOEI*.
Stockholm.

___   (2009). *OEI #46-47 - PROSA*.
Stockholm.

___   (2009). *POETRY (July/August 2009)*. Chicago: Poetry Foundation.

___   (2010). *OEI #48-50 - LudOEI*.
Stockholm.

___   (2010-01-00). *Das blaue Buch der Weissheit*. 112 pages. Bern:
edition taberna kritika. ISBN
9783905846096.

___   (2011). *OEI #52 - SV KONC KONS*.
Stockholm.

___   (2011). *OEI #53-54 - DDDD*.
Stockholm.

___   (2011). *OEI #55 - ON TAPE*.
Stockholm.

___   (2012). *OEI #58 - Sömn*.
Stockholm.

___   (2012). *OEI #59 - Arbete pågår 2*.
Stockholm.

___   (2013). *OEI #62 - ON PAPER*.
Stockholm.

___   (2013-01-00). *Corrected Slogans: Reading and Writing Conceptualism*.
268 pages. Triple Canopy and MCA
Denver. ISBN 9780984734627.

___   (2014). *OEI #66 - POEMA/PROCESSO*.
Stockholm.

___   (2014). *Please Add This To The List: Teaching Bernadette Mayer's*

Sonnets. 66 pages. New York: Tender Buttons Press. ISBN 9780927920087. [also see: Mayer, Bernadette.]

__ (2015). *ha!art 50 2/2015. Numer specjalny konceptualny.* Kraków.

__ (2015). *OEI #67-68 - Icke-bekräftande skrivande! / Scrittura non assertiva!.* Stockholm.

Aasprong, Monica (2003). *Soldatmarkedet.* Bergen: Biblioteket Gasspedal.

Abel, Jordan (2015-04-24). *Un/inhabited.* 240 pages. Vancouver: Talonbooks. ISBN 9780889229228.

Abendschein, Hartmut (2008). *Bibliotheca Caelestis. Tiddlywikiroman.* Bern: edition taberna kritika. ISBN 9783905846027.

Abendschein, Hartmut (2013-07-00). *Schellendiskursli / Schellenexkursli.* 92 pages. Bern: edition taberna kritika. ISBN 9783905846249.

Abendschein, Hartmut (2014-07-00). *Recycling Le Tour de France.* 72 pages. Bern: edition taberna kritika. ISBN 9783905846317.

Abendschein, Hartmut (2015-05-00). *Flarf Disco.* 98 pages. Bern: edition taberna kritika. ISBN 9783905846348.

Abendschein, Hartmut (2016-09-00). *Mein Jahr in Besorgungen*. 100 pages. edition taberna kritika.

Abish, Walter (1974). *Alphabetical Africa*. 168 pages. New York: New Directions. ISBN 0811205339.

Abish, Walter (1990). *99: The New Meaning*. 112 pages. Providence: Burning Deck Press. ISBN 0930901673.

Abramowitz, Harold (2010-06-01). *Not Blessed*. 86 pages. Los Angeles: Les Figues Press. ISBN 9781934254134.

Abramowitz, Harold (2015-02-19). *Writing dvic*. 149 pages. Gauss PDF.

[Abramowitz, Harold, and Richert, Dan] (2011-11-00). *(!x==[33]) Book 1 Volume 1 by .UNFO*. 776 pages. Los Angeles: Insert Blanc Press. ISBN 9780981462394.

[Abramowitz, Harold, and Richert, Dan] (2014-01-00). *(!x==[33]) Book 2 Volume 3 by .UNFO*. 776 pages. Los Angeles: Insert Blanc Press. ISBN 9780991109210.

[Abramowitz, Harold, and Richert, Dan] (2014-01-08). *UNFO Burns A Million Dollars*. [1519 pages]. Gauss PDF.

Abreu, Manuel Arturo (2014-06-03). *Selections from my VirtualDJ history*. [35 pages]. Gauss PDF.

Aby, Maddy (2014-02-12). *Reflections*. [60 pages]. Zürich: LUMA Foundation (1000 BOOKS BY 1000 POETS). ISBN 9781312009295.

Acconci, Vito (2006-03-00). [see Dworkin, Craig, ed. (2006-03-00).]

Acconci, Vito, and Mayer, Bernadette (2006-01-12). *0 TO 9: The Complete Magazine*: 1967-1969. 736 pages. New York: Ugly Duckling Presse. ISBN 9781933254203.

Acker, Kathy (1975/1978?). *The Adult Life of Toulouse Lautrec by Henri Toulouse Lautrec*. 201 pages. New York: TVRT.

Acker, Kathy (1983). *Great Expectations: A Novel*. 128 pages. New York: Grove Press. ISBN 9780394624808.

Ackerman, Amanda (2015-07-14). *The Book of Feral Flora*. 196 pages. Los Angeles: Les Figues Press. ISBN 9781934254585.

Adair, Danielle (2009). *From JBAD, Lessons Learned*. 80 pages. Los Angeles: Les Figues Press.

Adams, Sara (2016-02-00). *Think Like a B: Erasure Poems from Donald Trump's Think Like a Billionaire*. 21 pages. SOd press.

Adams, Scott (2012). *My Crobe*. [511 pages]. Gauss PDF.

Adams, Breton (2015-03-29). *A (meta) love story*. 125 pages. Homestead Press.

Adlers, Bengt (2013-10-15). *Novelties*. 136 pages. Stockholm: OEI editör. ISBN 9789185905621.

Akhbari, Rouzbeh (2013-10-14). *A Thousand Words is Six Hundred Thousand and Two Hundred Eighty Five Characters, based on a dialogue between François Côté and Benjamin Verdicchio*. 457 pp. Toronto: publishers&. ISBN 9781304532664.

Akhbari, Rouzbeh (2013-11-03). *Logical Determinism*. 202 pages. Toronto: publishers&. ISBN 9781304592187.

Akhbari, Rouzbeh (2013-11-03). *Logical Determinism (2)*. 203 pages. Toronto: publishers&. ISBN 9781304592040.

Alatalo, Sally [Anita M-28] (2001). *Unforeseen Alliances*. 136 pages. Chicago: Sara Ranchouse Publishing. ISBN 188863619X.

Alemian, Ezequiel (2010). *El libro blanco de la revista Time*. Buenos Aires: Spiral Jetty.

Alemian, Ezequiel (2010). *El tratado contra el método de Paul Feyerabend*. Buenos Aires: Spiral Jetty.

Alexander, Chris (2011). *PANDA*. 215 pages. Sunnyside, NY: Truck Books. [2nd edition in (2012); 280 pages. ISBN 9780984885725.]

Alexander, Chris, Copp, Corina, Fiterman, Rob, Gallagher, Kristen, Crawford, Alejandro, Kaplan, Josef, Fraga, Sophia Le, Melgard, Holly, Sylvester, Chris, Talone, Bridget, Yearous-Algozin, and Zultanski, Steve (2015-11-24). *SLOBJECT*. 448 pages. TROLL THREAD.

Allan, Liz, and MacKenzie, Perri (2015-05-00). *A Recent Writing*. 28 pages. Rotterdam: Back Door Books/Publication Studio. ISBN 9789492308030.

Alland, Sandra (2007-03-00). *Blissful Times*. 77 pages. Toronto: BookThug. ISBN 9780978158767.

Almonte, Carlos, y Meller, Alan (2001). *Neoconceptualismo. El Secuestro del Origen*. 97 pages. Delhi: Sarak Editions.

Almonte, Carlos, y Meller, Alan (2015). *Neoconceptualismo. Ensayos*. Delhi: Sarak Editions. ISBN 9789563583526.

Amino, Genji (2014-02-27). *The Populating Of The Field*. [354 pages]. Zürich: LUMA Foundation (1000 BOOKS BY 1000 POETS). ISBN 9781312056350.

aND, mIEKAL (1982). *Klee*. West Lima: Xerox Sutra Editions.

aND, mIEKAL (1983). *Zerzerex*. 128 pages. West Lima: Xerox Sutra Editions.

aND, mIEKAL (2016-12-12). *the Mina Loyalties*. 78 pages. West Lima: Xerox Sutra Editions. ISBN 9781936687350.

Andersen, Paal Bjelke (2008). *Til folket (2000-2008)*. 20 pages. Oslo: Flamme Forlag. ISBN 9788202297237.

Andersen, Paal Bjelke (2010). *Dugnad*. 192 pages. Oslo: Flamme Forlag. ISBN 9788202338916.

Andersen, Paal Bjelke (2010). *The Grefsen Address*. 192 pages. Helsinki: ntamo. ISBN 9789522151209.

Andersen, Paal Blejke (2010-03-27). *NAVNET - et dikt, for høytlesning på dansk og norsk*. Århus: Edition After Hand. ISBN 9788787489584.

Anderson, Erik (2010-06-01). *The Poetics of Trespass*. 104 pages. Los Angeles: Otis Books | Seismicity Editions. ISBN 9780979617775.

Anderson, Holly (2012-05-00). *The Night She Slept With A Bear*. 56 pages. Portland: Jank Editions/Publication Studio. ISBN

9781935662013. [Includes CD with music by Chris Brokaw.]

Andrews, Bruce (1999). *Peril.* TextThirtyOne (Potes & Poets).

Andrews, Bruce (2006). *WhDiP, a sequence from White Dialect Poetry.* 444 pages. /ubu editions (Publishing the Unpublishable).

Andrews, Bruce (2006). *Libretto, from White Dialect Poetry.* 165 pages. /ubu editions (Publishing the Unpublishable).

Andrews, Bruce, Bernstein, Charles, DiPalma, Ray, McCaffery, Steve, and Silliman, Ron (1980). *LEGEND.* 244 pages. New York: L=A=N=G=U=A=G=E/Segue Foundation.

Ang, Brian (2014-03-00). *[PARROT 21] Pre-Symbolic.* 20 pages. Los Angeles: Insert Blanc Press. ISSN 2169381121.

Angle, Renne (2016-04-01). *WoO.* 116 pages. Tucson: Letter Machine Editions. ISBN 9780988713765.

Antin, David (1991-04-00). *Selected Poems: 1963-1973* (Sun & Moon Classics). 431 pages. Los Angeles: Sun & Moon Press. ISBN 9781557130587.

Anzuoni, Michael (2014). *Anyone Within A 5 Mile Radius Who Is Single and Smokes / Musings of the Bot Chuck_Kinbote.* [2 volumes; 106, 20 pages]. Gauss PDF.

Anzuoni, Michael (2016-07-19). *a river babbles also*. [12 pages]. Gauss PDF.

Apps, Stan (2011-04-01). *The World as Phone Bill*. 248 pages. Cumberland, RI: Combo Books. ISBN 9780972888042.

aragão, antónio (1968). *mais exactamente p(r)o(bl)emas*. [74 pages]. Funchal: colecção pedras brancas.

aragão, antónio (1975). *os bancos antes da nacionalização*. [3],109 pages. Funchal.

Archer, Sacha (2016-04-00). *Dishwashing Event PART ONE: TIANJIN, CHINA*. Calgary: No press.

Ardis, James (2016-10-04). *Your Arkansas: A Strategy Guide*. [22 pages]. Gauss PDF.

Armstrong, Kate (2012-05-00). *Path: A Generative Bookwork in Twelve Volumes*. 12 volumes; 7300 pages. Vancouver: Publication Studio and UNIT/PITT Projects. ISBN 9781927394045. [Includes 168-hour mp3 audiobook edition on SD card.]

Arseguel, Gérard (2003-11-10). *Le journal du bord de terre*. 77 pages. Paris: Virgile. ISBN 9782908007633.

Arterian, Diana (2013-09-01). *Death Cantos*. 24 pages. New York: Ugly Duckling Presse.

Austin, Nathan (2009). *Survey Says!*. 61 pages. New York: Black Maze Books. ISBN 9780578011721.

AUTUMN ROYAL, CAHILL, MICHELLE, DALE, AMELIA, FLEMING, JOAN, GOMEZ, ELENA, NASHAR, CLAIRE, AND MACCARTHER, KENT (2016-08-04). *EXOSTALE CHRESTOMATHY*. [40 pages]. SOd press.

Avasilichioaei, Oana, and Moure, Erín (2009-09-00). *Expeditions of a Chimæra*. 96 pages. Toronto: BookThug. ISBN 9781897388470.

Babstock, Ken (2014-04-25). *SIGINT*. Calgary: No press.

Bajohr, Hannes (2015-05-13). *Erotica*. 62 pages. 0x0a.

Balestrini, Nanni (2014-01-00). *Tristano. A Novel*; translated by Mike Harakis, introduction by Umberto Eco. 128 pages. Verso Books. ISBN 9781781681695.

Ballard, J.G (1970). *The Atrocity Exhibition*. 157 pages. [London]: Doubleday & Company. ISBN 0224618385.

Ballesta, Alba (2014-03-01). *Clara Dubasenca Obras Completas Tomo III*. [96 pages].Zürich: LUMA Foundation (1000 BOOKS BY 1000 POETS). ISBN 9781312539921.

Bamfield, Peter (2012). *Un Hommage à Thomas Pynchon's Rainbow*. [30 pages]. Editions Eclipse.

Banner, Fiona (1997). *The Nam*. [1000 pages]. London: Frith Street Gallery. ISBN 9780951495315.

Banner, Fiona (2009). *ISBN 978-1-907118-92-0*. London: The Vanity Press. ISBN 9781907118920.

Banner, Fiona (2011). *Nude Film*. 12 pages. London: The Vanity Press.

Barber, Stephanie (2013-02-12). *Night Moves*. 86 pages. Atlanta: Publishing Genius Press. ISBN 9780988750302.

Barnwell, Jake (2014-02-17). *Addled Powers, Ale Powders*. [16/24 blank pages]. Zürich: LUMA Foundation (1000 BOOKS BY 1000 POETS). ISBN 9781312024250.

Barwin, Gary (2014-10-21). *NASA JPG: Earth View from the Top*. Calgary: Spacecraft Press.

Barwin, Gary (2015-08-26). *Servants of Dust*. [80 pages]. Gauss PDF.

barwin, gary, & beaulieu, derek (2005). *frogments from the frag pool: haiku after basho*. 112 pages. Toronto: The Mercury Press.

Basara, Robert, Belasco, Leonardo, Irwin, Jed, and Levy, William, eds. (1965). *The Insect Trust Gazette, Summer 1965. Philadelphia*. [relevant text: Coolidge, Clark. *Bond Sonnets*.]

Bataille, Georges, Leiris, Michel, Griauel, Marcel, Einstein, Carl, and Desnos, Robert, eds. (1995-12-00). *Encyclopaedia Acephalica, Atlas Arkhive (Book 3): Documents of the Avant-Garde*. 176 pages. London: Atlas Press. ISBN 0947745872.

Baum, Erica (2010). *Sightings*. 150 pages. Paris: onestar press.

Baum, Erica (2011-04-01). *Dog Ear*. [72 pages]. New York: Ugly Duckling Presse. ISBN 9781933254715.

Baum, Erica (2015-01-00). *The Man from U.N.C.L.E*. Calgary: No press.

bäcker, heimrad (1986). *nachschrift*. 142 pages. Linz: edition neue texte.

bäcker, heimrad (1997-01-00). *nachschrift 2*. 264 pages. Graz: literaturverlag droschl (edition neue texte). ISBN 9783854204725.

Bäcker, Heimrad (2013-11-01). *SEASCAPE*, translated by Patrick Greaney. 20 pages. New York: Ugly Duckling Presse. [Original text: *Seestück*, published as issue 32 of the journal Neue Texte, Linz, 1985.]

Bäcker, Heimrad (2014-02-02). *Documentary Poetry*; translated by Jacquelyn Deal and Patrick Greaney. Calgary: No press.

Bean, Victoria, and McCabe, Chris, ed. (2015-09-29). *The New*

Concrete: Visual Poetry in the 21st Century. 240 pages. London: Hayward Publishing. ISBN 9781853323287.

Beard, Steve (1998). *Perfumed Head*. 92 pages. London: Book Works. ISBN 9781870699303.

Beauchamp, Rebecca (2015-12-29). *Welcome to My Book*. [9 pages]. Gauss PDF.

Beaulieu, Derek (2007). *Flatland: a romance of many dimensions*. 110 pages. York: information as material. ISBN 9780955309250.

Beaulieu, Derek (2008). *How To Write/How To Edit*. 54 pages. /ubu editions (Publishing the Unpublishable).

beaulieu, derek, ed. (2008-07-00). *LEGO 50-15*. Calgary: No press.

beaulieu, derek (2008-10-13). *Local Colour*. 80 pages. Helsinki: ntamo. ISBN 9789522150493.

beaulieu, derek, ed. (2009). *26 Alphabets (for Sol LeWitt)*. 60 pages. Calgary: No press.

beaulieu, derek (2009). *wild rose country*. Ottawa: above/ground press.

beaulieu, derek (2010-01-00). *Colour*. [16 pages]. Calgary: No press. [2nd edition: (2011). Vernon, BC: twenty-two press.]

beaulieu, derek (2010-03-31). *How to Write*. 72 pages. Vancouver: talonbooks. ISBN 9780889226296.

beaulieu, derek (2011). *seen of the crime: essays*. 88 pages. Montreal: Snare Books. ISBN 9780986576546.

beaulieu, derek, ed. (2011-06-00). *ubu à cinquante*. Calgary: No press.

beaulieu, derek (2012). [Rabble]. *All Work and No Play Makes Jack a Dull Boy*. [8 pages]. Los Angeles: Insert Blanc Press. ISSN 21687439.

beaulieu, derek (2013-02-00). [see Dobson, Kit, ed. (2013-02-00).]

beaulieu, derek (2015). *Game of Life: A User's Manual*. [4 pages]. Calgary: Spacecraft Press.

beaulieu, derek (2015-11). *The Unbearable Contact with Poets*. 120 pages. Manchester: if p then q. ISBN 9780957182783.

beaulieu, derek (2016-02-05). *Erasing Warhol*. [4 pages]. Calgary: Spacecraft Press.

beaulieu, derek (2016-03-00). *a a novel*. 8 pages. Calgary: No press. [Excerpt from an edition due to be released (2017). Paris: Jean Boîte Editions.]

beaulieu, derek (2016-05-00). *La Disparition*. 1 page. Calgary: No press.

beaulieu, derek (2016-11-00). *Quercus: "Nations hurled together so they might learn to know one another"*. 2 pages. Ottawa: above/ground press.

beaulieu, derek, and Emerson, Lori, eds. (2013). *Writing Surfaces: Selected Fiction of John Riddell*. 158 pages. Waterloo: Wilfrid Laurier University Press. ISBN 9781554588282.

Beaulieu, Derek, Lindh, Carl, & Ståhl, Ola (2012-12-20). *Local Colour; ghosts, variations*. [paperback volumes, book of photographs, CD and software]. Malmö: Publication Studio Malmö / In Edit Mode Press. ISBN 9789197785341.

beaulieu, derek, and mclennan, rob, eds. (2016-11-01). *The Calgary Renaissance*. 250 pages. Calgary: Chaudiere Books. ISBN 9781928107071.

Beckett, Samuel (1951). *Molloy*. 298 pages. Paris: Les Éditions de Minuit.

Beckett, Samuel (1953). *Watt*. 254 pages. Paris: Olympia Press.

Beckman, Joshua, McCann, Anthony, and Rohrer, Matthew (2007). *Gentle Reader!*. 68 pages. Seattle: Wave Books.

Beckwith, Caleb, ed. (2015-11-00). *Reconfiliating: Conversations with Conceptual-Affiliated Writers* (with J. Gordon Faylor, Danny Snelson and Divya Victor and an afterword by Joseph Mosconi). 74 pages. Essay Press.

Beckwith, Caleb (2016-07-04). *Hi, You're Beautiful.* [45 pages]. Gauss PDF.

Belgum, Erik (2009). *THE_CITY Battery, a Neurological Evaluation of THE_CITY.* 49 pages. /ubu editions (Publishing the Unpublishable).

Bellamy, Dodie (2001-10-01). *Cunt-Ups.* 67 pages. New York: Tender Buttons Press. ISBN 9780927920094.

Bellamy, Dodie (2013-11-19). *Cunt Norton.* 75 pages. Los Angeles: Les Figues Press. ISBN 9781934254493.

Benenson, Fred, ed. (2010-09-07). *Emoji Dick; or,* 🐳 *by Herman Melville, translated by Amazon Mechanical Turk.* 736 pages. Lulu.

Benjamin, Walter (1983). *Das Passagen-Werk.* 1354 pages. Berlin: Suhrkamp Verlag. ISBN 9783518112007.

Bennett, Guy (2011-04-05). *Self-Evident Poems.* 96 pages. Los Angeles: Otis Books | Seismicity Editions. ISBN 9780984528905.

Bennett, Guy, and Vangelisti, Paul, eds. (2008-08-15). *Signs/ & Signals: the Daybooks of Robert Crosson*. 245 pages. Los Angeles: Otis Books | Seismicity Editions. ISBN 9780979617737.

Benson, Cara (2016-05-15). *Let Me Be Clear*. New York: Ugly Duckling Presse.

Bentley, A(mel)ia (2014-10-20). *Obstacle, Particle, Spectacle*. [148 pages]. Zürich: LUMA Foundation (1000 BOOKS BY 1000 POETS). ISBN 9781312614178.

Bercik, Brendan R. (2014-03-16). *Tracing*. [106 pages]. Zürich: LUMA Foundation (1000 BOOKS BY 1000 POETS). ISBN 9781304978578.

Berge, Gunnar (2011). *Claude X-faktoren*. 58 pages. Oslo: Forlaget Attåt. ISBN 9788293029052.

Bergvall, Caroline (1996). *Éclat*. London: Sound & Language. ISBN 9781899100064.

Bergvall, Caroline (2005). *Fig (Goan Atom 2)*. 148 pages. Cambridge: Salt Publishing. ISBN 9781844710928.

Bergvall, Caroline (2011-02-00). *Meddle English: New and Selected Texts*. 176 pages. Callicoon: Nightboat Books. ISBN 9780982264584.

Bergvall, Caroline, Browne, Laynie, Carmody, Teresa, and Place, Vanessa, eds. (2012-04-17). *I'll Drown My Book: Conceptual Writing by Women*. 455 pages. Los Angeles: Les Figues Press. ISBN 9781934254332.

Bergvall, Caroline, & Thurston, Nick (2009). *The Die is Cast*. 16 pages. York: information as material. ISBN 9780955309298.

Bernstein, Charles (1975). *Asylums*. [50 pages]. New York: Asylum's Press.

Bernstein, Charles (1976). *Parsing*. [50 pages]. New York: Asylum's Press.

Bernstein, Charles (1987). *The Sophist*. 179 pages. Los Angeles: Sun & Moon Press. ISBN 9780940650794.

Bernstein, Charles (1987-03-00). *Veil*. 12 pages. West Lima: Xcxoxial Editions.

Bernstein, Charles (2008). *Three Works*. 7 pages. /ubu editions (Publishing the Unpublishable).

Bernstein, Charles (2012-11-29). *Last Words from 'Sentences My Father Used'*. Calgary: No press.

Bernstein, Felix (2015-06-00). *Notes on Post-Conceptual Poetry*. 170 pages. Los Angeles: Insert Blanc Press. ISBN 9780996169639.

Bernstein, Felix (2016-02-02). *Burn Book*. 128 pages. Callicoon: Nightboat Books. ISBN 9781937658427.

Bernstein, Michèle (2012). *Alla kungens hästar*. 80 pages. Stockholm: OEI editör. ISBN 9789185905362.

Berrigan, Ted, Brainard, Joe, and Padgett, Ron (1967). *Bean Spasms*. 202 pages. New York: Kulchur Press.

Bervin, Jen (2004). *Nets*. 130 pages. New York: Ugly Duckling Presse. ISBN 9780972768436.

Bervin, Jen (2008). *The Desert*. 148 pages. New York: Granary Books.

Betts, Gregory (2000). *All You Need to Know*. House Press.

Betts, Gregory (2005-10-00). *If Language*. 107 pages. Toronto: BookThug. ISBN 9780973718164.

Big, Sebastian (2015-11-00). *Vată de sticlă*. 70 pages. Bistrița: Editura Charmides. ISBN 9786067520200.

Big, Sebastian (2016-11-18). *Masiv*. [32 pages]. București: frACTalia. ISBN 9786069428528.

Bilyk, Volodymyr (2016). *undestanding (of language) are not enough / la compresione (del linguaggio) non basta* (translated by Ermanno Moretti). 94 pages. Diaforia.

bissett, bill (1971). *Rush: what fuckan theory; a study uv language*. Toronto: grOnk; Vancouver: blewointment, nd.

Blachly, Jimbo, and Shaw, Lytle (2008-10-15). *The Chadwick Family Papers (A Brief Public Glimpse)*. 175 pages. Periscope. ISBN 9781934772904.

Blake, Nayland (2008-03-00). *Also Also Also Rises The Sun*. Calgary: No press. [Also see Fitterman, Robert (2008-03-00).]

Boglione, Riccardo (2009). *Ritmo D. Feeling the Blanks*. 116 pages. Montevideo: gegen.

Boglione, Riccardo, ed. (2011). *Crux Desperationis 1*. Montevideo: gegen.

Boglione, Riccardo, ed. (2012-04-12). *Crux Desperationis 2 (mental issue)*. Montevideo: gegen.

Boglione, Riccardo, ed. (2012-12-00). *Crux Desperationis 3*. Montevideo: gegen.

Boglione, Riccardo (2013). *The Perfect Library*. 80 pages. Montevideo: gegen.

Boglione, Riccardo, ed. (2013-09-00). *Crux Desperationis 4 (mental issue)*. Montevideo: gegen.

Boglione, Riccardo, ed. (2014-01-00). *Crux Desperationis 5*. Montevideo: gegen.

Boglione, Riccardo, ed. (2014-12-00). *Crux Desperationis 6 (mental issue)*. Montevideo: gegen.

Boglione, Riccardo, ed. (2015-10-00). *Crux Desperationis 7*. Montevideo: gegen.

Boglione, Riccardo, ed. (2016-07-00). *Crux Desperationis 8 (mental issue)*. Montevideo: gegen.

Bory, Jean-François (2007-01-00). *Bienvenue Monsieur Gutenberg*. 20 pages. Bordeaux: Éditions de l'Attente. ISBN 9782914688567.

Borzutzky, Daniel (2015). *Memories of my Overdevelopment*. 64 pages. Chicago: Kennings Editions.

Botten, Katherine (2014-02-27). *Positive Trauma*. [76 pages]. Zürich: LUMA Foundation (1000 BOOKS BY 1000 POETS). ISBN 9781312056800.

BOWEN, JEREMIAH RUSH (2012-02-27). *NAZI: argument on the internet (5/31/11 – 8/31/11), v.1*. 390 pages. TROLL THREAD.

BOWEN, JEREMIAH RUSH (2012-02-27). *FAGGOT: argument on the internet (5/31/11 – 8/31/11), v.2*. 380 pages. TROLL THREAD.

Bök, Christian (1994). *Crystallography (Information*

Theory, Book 1). 114 pages. Toronto: Coach House Press. ISBN 0889104964. [2nd edition, revised: Bök, Christian (2003). *Crystallography*. 160 pages. Toronto: Coach House Press. ISBN 1552451194.]

Bök, Christian (2000). *String Variables*. housepress / CrO2. ISBN 9781894174312.

Bök, Christian (2001-10-20). *Eunoia*. 112 pages. Toronto: Coach House Books. ISBN 1552450929. [also: (2009-10-00). *Eunoia. The Upgraded Edition*. 120 pages. Toronto: Coach House Books. ISBN 9781552452257.]

Bök, Christian (2007). *The Xenotext Experiment*. 10 pages. /ubu editions (Publishing the Unpublishable).

Bök, Christian (2009). *Two Dots over a Vowel*. Calgary: No press.

Bök, Christian (2015-10-20). *The Xenotext: Book 1*. 160 pages. Toronto: Coach House Books. ISBN 9781552453216.

Börjel, Ida (2006). *Skåneradio*. 107 pages. Stockholm: Modernista. ISBN 9789197601429.

Börjel, Ida (2008-04). *Konsumentköplagen: juris lyrik*. 198 pages. Stockholm: OEI editör. ISBN 9789185905010.

bpNichol (1968). *The Complete Works*. Toronto: GANGLIA PRESS.

bpNichol, ed. (1970). *The Cosmic Chef: An Evening of Concrete*. Oberon Press. ISBN 0887500242.

bpNichol (1979). *Translating Translating Apollinaire: A Preliminary Report*. 46 pages. Milwaukee: Membrane Press. [New edition edited by CAConrad out soon on Nightboat, ISBN 9781937658120.]

Brafmann, Adam (2014). *Bestseller*. [88 pages and additional MP4 file]. Gauss PDF.

Braun, Victoria (2014-03-18). *#girlproblems*. [58 pages]. Zürich: LUMA Foundation (1000 BOOKS BY 1000 POETS). ISBN 9781304954442.

Briggs, Kate (2013-12-00). *On reading as an alternation of flights and perchings*. Calgary: No press.

Brooks-Motl, Hannah (2015-12-00). *M.* 96 pp. The Song Cave. ISBN 9780996778602.

Brown, Brandon (2012-11-20). *FLOWERING MALL*. 112 pages. New York: Roof Books. ISBN 978931824484.

Brown, Brandon (2014-10-00). *Top 40*. 136 pages. New York: Roof Books. ISBN 9781931824576.

Browne, Laynie (2007-02-00). *Daily Sonnets*. 176 pages. Denver: Counterpath Press. ISBN 9781933996004.

Browne, Susanna (2011-05-25). *Country War Songs*. 76 pages. Vancouver: Bookmachine/Publication Studio. ISBN 9780986676352.

Brox, Robin F., & aND, mIEKAL (2012). *of fracture. rewriting Factura by Bruce Andrews*. 52 pages. Xerox Sutra Editions. ISBN 9781936687084.

Buck, Marie (2007-09-00). *Life & Style*. 10 pages. Chicago: Beard of Bees Press.

Buck, Paul (2015-03-06). *To End It All*. 32 pages. London: Test Centre.

Bucur, Anca, Militaru, Iulia, şi Rotaru, Andra, antlg. (2016-10-00). *O formă capricioasă de poezie (antologie)* [ilustraţii: Cristina Florentina Budar]. 144 pp. Bucureşti: frACTalia. ISBN 9786069400593.

Buddeus, Ondřej (2011). *55 007 znaků včetně mezer*. Praha: Petr Štengl. ISBN 9788090445574.

"Buerhaus, Cammisa" [Compiled by the Presidential Correspondence Intern Cammisa Buerhaus] (2015-12-01). *Hillary Clinton's Private Emails and Memos as Read by Debbie Harry* at the *Benghazi Hearing*. [12 pages]. Gauss PDF.

Bulloch, Angela (2000). *Rule Book*. 128 pages. London: Book Works. ISBN 9781870699440.

Burda, Vladimir, translated by jwcurry (1992-02-20). *ich: 4 translations of Vladimir Burda*. Toronto.

Burger, Mary, Glück, Robert, Roy, Camille, and Scott, Gail, eds. (2004-10-00). *Biting the Error. Writers Explore Narrative*. 304 pages. Toronto: Coach House Books. ISBN 9781552451427.

Burke, Harry, ed. (2014-04-16). *I Love Roses When They're Past Their Best*. 137 pages. London: PWR Studio/Test Centre. ISBN 9780992685836.

Burnham, Clint (2009-04-00). *The Benjamin Sonnets*. 62 pp. Toronto: BookThug. ISBN 9781897388365.

Burr, Tom (2015-11-00). [see Deriuex, Florence (2015-11-00)].

Burrau, Elis (2014-02-13). *om dig har alla sagt det som inte borde ha sagts att en sötnos är nos som är söt så går den*. [116 pages]. Zürich: LUMA Foundation (1000 BOOKS BY 1000 POETS). ISBN 9781312012745.

Burroughs, William S. (1964). *Nova Express*. 187 pages. New York: Grove Press.

Burroughs, William S., and Gysin, Brion (1978). *The Third Mind*. i-vi; 194 pages. New York: Viking Press.

Burton, Pascale (2016-04-00). *the death of the author (after Roland Barthes)*. [28 pages]. SOd press.

Bury, Louis (2015). *Exercices in Criticism: The Theory and Practice of Literary Constraint*. Champaign: Dalkey Archive Press. ISBN 9781628971057.

Buuck, David, & Spahr, Juliana (2013-09-22). *An Army of Lovers*. 150 pages. San Francisco: City Lights Publishers. ISBN 9780872866294.

Büchler, Pavel (2004). *The Answer to the Question*. 16 pages. York: information as material. ISBN 0953676560.

Bülhoff, Andreas (2015-09-03). *VOXEL POEM*. Calgary: Spacecraft Press.

Bülhoff, Andreas (2016-08-25). *die außenwelt der innenwelt der außenwelt*. 14 pages. Köln: parasitenpresse.

Byrne, Mairéad (2007). *SOS Poetry*. 85 pages. /ubu editions.

Cadiot, Olivier (1988). *L'art poetic'*. 231 pages. Paris: P.O.L. ISBN 2867445558.

Cage, John (1969). *A Year from Monday: New Lectures and Writings*. Middletown: Wesleyan University Press.

Cage, John (1973-03-15). *M: Writings '67-'72*. 233 pages. Middletown: Wesleyan University Press. ISBN 9780819560353.

Cage, John (1979-02-00): *Empty Words: Writings '73-'78*. 199 pp. Middletown: Wesleyan University Press. ISBN 9780819560674.

Cage, John (1983). *X: Writings '79-'82*. 187 pages. Middletown: Wesleyan University Press. ISBN 0819550906.

Cain, Buffy (2015-01-00). *(n+1)+1: The Decivilizing Process Server*. [198 pages]. GPDF Editions.

Callanan, Martin John (2007). *Letters 2004-2006: Confirmation That You Still Exist; I Respect Your Authority; When Will It End: One London*. 48 pages. London: Book Works. ISBN 9781870699983.

Calle, Sophie (1998-12-00). *Le Carnet d'adresses (Livre VI)*. 18 pages. Editeur Actes-sud. ISBN 2742718699.

Camil, Camil L.A. (2014). *şA(n)seLe din 49 (piese de poezie)*. [116 pages]. București: Tracus Arte. ISBN 9786066642422.

Capone, Francesca (2015-06-15). *Primary Source*. [240 pages]. GPDF Editions.

Carr, Angela (2009-11-00). *The Rose Concordance*. 96 pages. Toronto: BookThug. ISBN 9781897388464.

Carreño, Juan (2014-03-01). *bomba bencina*. [74 pages]. Zürich: LUMA Foundation (1000 BOOKS BY 1000 POETS). ISBN 9781304907509.

Carrión, Ulises (1972). *Sonnet(s)*. [45 pages]. Amsterdam: In-Out Productions.

Carrión, Ulises (1973). *Arguments*. 86 pages. Cullompton: Beau Geste Press.

Carrión, Ulises (2010). *Gossip, Scandal and Good Manners [1981]*. 52 pages. London: Fraser Muggeridge Studio.

Carrión, Ulises (2016). *(a, b, c)*. [24/24 blank pages]. Geneva: Boabooks.

Carrión, Ulises (2016). *rrr*. [24 pages]. Geneva: Boabooks.

Carrión, Ulises (2016). *(the drum)*. [24 pages]. Geneva: Boabooks.

Carruthers, A.J. (2016-08-24). *Opus 16 on Tehching Hsieh*. [100 pages]. Gauss PDF.

Carstensen, Claus (2015-05-27). *Terr*. Århus: Antipyrine. ISBN 9788793108257

Castillejo, José Luis (1969). *The Book of i's*. [400 pages]. [Germany].

Cayley, John (2015-07-00). *Image Generation*. London: Veer Books. ISBN 9781907088827

Cazal, Philippe (2000). *Les Litanies*. Chatou.

Cearley, Sean (2015-09-03). *The Travesties of Plato*. Calgary: Spacecraft Press.

Cendrars, Blaise (1924). *Kodak (Documentaire)*. 95 pages. Paris: Librairie Stock.

Cesarco, Alejandro (2003-09-00). *Dedications*. Montevideo/New York: a.r.t. press.

Cha, Theresa Hak Kyung (1982). *Dictee*. 179 pages. New York: Tanam Press. ISBN 0934378096.

Chanel, Anne-Laure (2012-11-00). *Luzern*. 12 pages. Clamart: Les Cahiers de la Seine.

Chodzko, Adam (2002). *Romanov*. 64 pages. London: Book Works. ISBN 9781870699518.

Christensen, Inger (1981). *alfabet*. 76 pages. Oslo: Lyrikbogklubben Borgen-Gyldendal. ISBN 8700471720.

Christoffel, David (2010-06-00). *Littéralicismes*. 78 pages.

Bordeaux: Éditions de l'Attente. ISBN 9782914688987.

Ciccone, Ray (2015-02-11). OCRGASM. [36 pages]. I barely know her. ISBN 5800108602169 [?].

Claburn, Thomas (2006-05-00). *i feel better after i type to you*. 254 pages. Superbunker.

Clair, Tonya St. (2012). *Cloud storage for everyone*. [5 pages]. Gauss PDF.

Clair, Tonya St. (2012). *Uncontrolled quantiative nullpropriation: a quasi-experiment and duplicate submission*. Gauss PDF.

Clark, Elisabeth S. (2007). *Between Words*. 62 pages. London: Atlas Press & [/ubu editions (Publishing the Unpublishable)].

claudel, matthew (2014-03-24). *Read?*. Zürich: LUMA Foundation (1000 BOOKS BY 1000 POETS). ISBN 9781312543669.

Clavel, Michel (2012-08-00). *de ma main gauche*. 32 pages. Bordeaux: Éditions de l'Attente. ISBN 9782362420283.

Closky, Claude (1989). *Les 1000 premiers nombres classés par ordre alphabétique*. [16 pages]. [Translated in Norwegian by Paal Bjelke Andersen; 2009-08-00; Oslo:

Forlaget Attåt. ISBN 9788293029014.]

Closky, Claude (1992). *Couché sur le ventre*. 15 [28] pages.

Closky, Claude (1992). *The 365 days of 1991 classified by size*. 16 pages. Paris.

Closky, Claude (1992). *Three thousand four hundred and fifteen Friday the 13ths*. 16 pages. Paris.

Closky, Claude (1999). *Mon Catalogue*. 288 pages. Limoges: Frac Limousin.

Closky, Claude (2006). *The 2007 calendar*. 80 pages. Paris: Galerie Laurent Godin/onestar press. ISBN 291535916229.

Coates, Marcus (2014). *UR... A Practical Guide to Unconscious Reasoning*. 320 pages. London: Book Works. ISBN 9781906012618.

Cobbing, Bob (1977). *Cygnet Ring: Collected Poems - Volume One*. [32 pages]. London: Tapocketa Press.

Cobbing, Bob (1978-04-00). *WAN / ABC / DO / TREE. Collected Poems, Volume Two*. [50 pages]. London: EL UEL UEL U Publications.

Cole, Norma (2006). *Collective Memory*. 52 pages. New York: Granary Books.

Coleman, Victor (2012-10-00). *ivH: An Alphamath Serial*. 96 pages.

Toronto: BookThug. ISBN 9781927040362.

Colombo, John Robert (1974). *Translations from the English: Found Poems.* 118 pp. Toronto: Peter Martin Associates.

Comitta, Tom (2013-11-06). *◯.* 59 pages. New York: Ugly Duckling Presse.

Comitta, Tom (2015-04-27). *First Thought Worst Thought: Collected Books 2011-2014. [A bundle of the following books: The Anniversary Show. I Can See You But I Know You're There. [cabinet]- equivalent) for approval, and that \ VOLTAIRE. Balding Type. Blueprint for Realist Cinema (Two Stars). point line shape. soUNDtext User's Manual. currents. anemone by Mot Ramrot. : 2011. (2011); badvertisements, or exercises in rerouting, confusing and eliminating desire. TEXT YES.pdf. waiting for godog. Summer on Nob Hill: Part 1. Summer on Nob Hill: Part 2. In the Time of the Leaves. P A R K in memoriam Mary Ellen Solt. 1948 by George Orwell. Z by Andy Warhol. PR: AN OPERA. Portrait of the Artist as an Unborn Child Star. ASAP's Fables by ASAP. Lorem Ipsum by Lorem Ipsum. The Happy End of The Happy*

End of Franz Kafka's Amerika. maybe failed texttile book.doc. Jurnes ut f the by Rert Mnre. ZIGZAG. On the Road Not Taken. To the Left and Right of the Lighthouse. Lettuce. Proposal for Partial Renovation of the Main Stairwell at 8 Samoset St., San Francisco, CA 94110 (37° 44' N / 122° 24' W). Haircut. : 2012. (2012); Story of the Dot. queer porn tv enterance (accidental book). O. : 2013. (2013); IN ITIBIIGRIPHI by Igir Strivinski. SENT. The Idiot. First Thought Worst Thought. ___ _____ __ _____. : 2014. (2014); Guide Book (2015)]. Gauss PDF.

Coolidge, Clark (1965). *Bond Sonnets* [see Basara, Robert et alii (1965)].

Coolidge, Clark (1968). *ING.* [54 pages.] New York: Angel Hair Books.

[Coolidge, Clark, and Fagin, Larry] (1973). *TONTO LAVORIS.* [16/18 blank pages]. New York: Adventures in Poetry.

Coppe, Alison (2015-12-00). *Split—I imagine you.* [11 pages]. SOd press.

Corrigan, Cecilia (2014-09-15). *TITANIC.* 176 pages. Lake Forest,

IL: Lake Forest College Press. ISBN 9781941423998.

Cory, Jean-Jacques [Kostelanetz, Richard] (1974). *Lists*. [32 pages]. Brooklyn, N.Y.: Assembling Press.

Covey, Bruce (2006-10-02). *Elapsing Speedway Organism*. 104 pages. Reston: No Tell Books LLC. ISBN 9781847283146.

Covey, Bruce (2010-10-06). *Glass Is Really a Liquid*. 142 pages. Reston: No Tell Books LLC. ISBN 9780982600016.

Coy, Chris (2014-01-20). *After Brad Troemel*. 288 pages. Brescia: LINK Editions. ISBN 9781291404098.

Crane, Hart (1933). *The Collected Poems of Hart Crane*. xxix, 180 pages. New York: Liveright Publishing Corporation. [relevant text: *Emblems of Conduct*]

Crawford, Alejandro Miguel Justino (2013-03-06). *poemfield3*. [590 pages + NAME + MOV files]. Gauss PDF.

Crews, Anna (2014-05-27). *Smart Casual*. [12 pages]. Gauss PDF.

Crosson, Robert (2008-08-15). [see Bennett, Guy, and Vangelisti, Paul, eds. (2008-08-15)].

Cuje (2013). *Untitled*. [22 pages + ZIP]. Gauss PDF.

Cussen, Felipe (2015-11-04). *Explicit Content*. [31 pages]. Gauss PDF.

Cussen, Felipe (2016). *Correcciones*. 3 volumes; 104, 38, 56 pages. information as material/Eclipse Archive.

Cussen, Felipe (2016-12-19). *Closed Caption*. [31 pages]. Gauss PDF.

Dale, Amelia (2015). *METADATA*. [67 pages]. STALE OBJECTS dePRESS [SOd press]. ISBN 5800107190681.

Dale, Amelia (2015-10-05). *Grumpy Cat 2 Reads Sanditon Chapter 2*. [9 pages]. Gauss PDF.

Dale, Amelia (2015-12-02). *TRACTOSAUR*. [40 pages]. TROLL THREAD.

Daly, Kieran (2010). *ANT OF A MISE EN SCENE*. [14 pages]. Gauss PDF.

Daly, Kieran (2010). *Live Cams*. [22 pages]. Gauss PDF.

Daly, Kieran (2014-02-12). ~~*Suspended (of) the formal capacity to sample and thereby preserve such samples according to the conditions from which they appeared*~~. [8; 32 blank pages]. Zürich: LUMA Foundation (1000 BOOKS BY 1000 POETS). ISBN 9781312009516.

Daly, Kieran (2014-11-25). *7 CLOSET DRAMAS*. [22 pages]. GPDF Editions.

Daly, Liza (2015-01-03). *Seraphs. A procedurely generated mysterious codex*. 72 pages. Blurb.

Danielewski, Mark Z. (2006-09-12). *Only Revolutions*. New York: Pantheon Books. ISBN 0375421769.

Darragh, Tina (1993). *adv. fans – the 1968 series*. [14 pages]. Buffalo: LEAVE books.

Darragh, Tina (2002-05-31). *from **rule of dumbs***. 8 pages. Brooklyn: Belladonna Books.

Darragh, Tina (2009-09-00). *opposable dumbs: a project report*. [33 pages]. Zimzalla.

Darragh, Tina, & Durand, Marcella (2009). *Deep eco pré*. 44 pages. LRL e-editions.

Daussin, Carolyn Nicole (2014-02-12). *Spiritual Education*. [30/32 blank pages]. Zürich: LUMA Foundation (1000 BOOKS BY 1000 POETS). ISBN 9781312009219.

Davenport, Philip, and Guest, Rebecca, eds. (2012-03-06). *TWEET FROM ENGELS*. 80 pages. Manchester: Apple Pie Editions. ISBN 9780956858481.

Davenport, Philip, ed. (2013-14-11). *The Dark Would: v. 1: Language Art Anthology*. 300 pages. Manchester: Apple Pie Publishing. ISBN 9781909388000.

David, Adam (2010-09-00). *The El Bimbo Variations*. 123 pages. The Youth & Beauty Brigade. ISBN 9789716918335.

Davies, Alan (1981). *a an av es*. [12/14 blank pages]. Needham: Potes & Poets Press.

Davies, Alan (1982-06-00). *Mnemonotechnics*. [30 pages]. Hartford: Potes & Poets Press.

Davies, Alan (2012-11-13). *Raw waR*. 102 pages. Honolulu: subpress collective. ISBN 9781930068612.

Davis, Brian Joseph (2007). *Voice Over*. 22 pages. /ubu editions (Publishing the Unpublishable).

Davis, Brian Joseph (2011-12-01). *The Consumed Guide*. 40 pages. Los Angeles: Insert Blanc Press.

De Francesco, Alessandro (2009). *da 1000m - dès 1000m - from 1000m*. Translations by the author, Noura Wedell, Doriane Bier, Laurent Prost and Caroline Zekri. 64 pages. HGH.

De Francesco, Alessandro (2016-02-03). *Remote Vision (poetry 1999-2015)*, Translated from the Italian by Belle Cushing and Dusty Neu. 342 pages. New York: Punctum Books. ISBN 9780692611340.

Dearden, Graeme (2014-09-23). *Shop Talk*. [64 pages]. Zürich: LUMA

Foundation (1000 BOOKS BY 1000 POETS). ISBN 9781312543928.

Debord, Guy, and Jorn, Asger (1959). *Mémoires*. [64 pages]. Copenhague: Éditions Situationist International.

Degentesh, Katie (2006-10-01). *The Anger Scale*. 75 pages. Cumberland, RI: Combo Books. ISBN 9780972888028.

Deisler, Guillermo (1972?). *Poemas visivos y proposiciones a realizar de...* [28 pages]. [Santiago del Chile]: Ediciones Mimbre.

Deisler, Guillermo (1992). *Milk (Found Poetry)*. Halle.

Deriuex, Florence (2015-11-00). *Tom Burr. Anthology: Writings 1991-2015*. 128 pages. Berlin: Sternberg Press/FRAC Champagne-Ardenne. ISBN 9783956791963.

Desjardin, Arnaud (2011). *Business As Usual*. 60 pages. Vancouver: Bookmachine/Publication Studio. ISBN 9780986676345.

Di Blasi, Debra (2007). *The Jirí Chronicles & Other Fictions. 192 pages. Tuscaloosa: FC2/University of Alabama Press*. ISBN 9781573661362.

Diderot, Denis (1796). *Jacques le fataliste et son maître*. xxij, 23-286 pages. Paris: Buisson.

DiMichele, Bill (1985). *Bilocations*. West Lima: Xexoxial Editions.

Dobson, Kit, ed. (2013-02-00). *Please, No More Poetry: The Poetry of derek beaulieu*. xvi; 74 pages. Waterloo: Wilfrid Laurier University Press. ISBN 9781554588299.

Doller, Sandra + Ben (2014). *Sonneteers*. [52 pages]. Editions Eclipse.

Donguy, Jacques (2007). *Poésies expérimentales – Zone numérique (1953-2007)*. 400 pages. Dijon: Les presses du réel. ISBN 9782840662020.

Donham, Housten (2015-07-14). *h&d*. [16 pages + MP3 file]. Gauss PDF.

Doris, Stacy (2000). *Paramour*. 138 pages. San Francisco: Krupskaya Books. ISBN 1928650058.

Doris, Stacy (2011-07-00). *The Cake Part*. 176 pages. Portland: Jank Editions/Publication Studio. ISBN 9781935662501.

DOWLING, SARAH (2012-10-25). *BIRDS & BEES*. [44 pages]. TROLL THREAD.

Dowling, Sarah (2014-11-11). *DOWN*. 88 pages. Toronto: Coach House. ISBN 9781552452981.

Drayton, Dave (2015-06-05). *Poetic Pentagrams*. Calgary: Spacecraft Press.

Drayton, Dave (2016-08-26). *HAITUROGRAMS*. [26 pages]. SOd press.

Dróżdż, Stanisław (2015). *Pojęciokształty. Poezja konkretna*. [editor: Andrzej Przywara]. 479 pages. Warszawa: Fundacja Galerii Foksal. ISBN 9788389302281.

Drucker, Johanna (1977). *FROM A TO Z: The Our An (Collective Specifics) an im partial bibliography, Incidents in a Non-relationship or: how I came to not know who is.* [66 pages]. Philadelphia: Chased Press.

Drucker, Johanna (2014-09-30). *DIAGRAMMATIC writing*. 36 pages. Eindhoven: Onomatopee. ISBN 9789491677120.

Duchamp, Marcel (1975). [see Sanouillet, Michel, and Peterson, Elmer, eds. (1975)]

dumond, frédéric (1995). *livre aidé («la copropriété»)*. 144 paqes.

dumond, frédéric (1997). *mots semblants*. 58 pages. Barcelona.

Dumond F[rédéric]. (1997-03-00). *La peuvresse comme véritrès affective de l'humme (aidé)*. Valence.

Dumond, Frédéric (1998). ***. 85 pages.

Dumond, Frédéric (1999). *Un yoyo dans un magasin*. 96 pages. Paris.

dumond, frédéric (2003). *fsyeofgaar ng*. 44 pages. Paris/Amsterdam.

dumond, frédéric (2004). *il est indispensable®* *(poèmes aidés)*. Bruxelles/Paris.

dumond, frédéric (2007-10-00). *téléologies*. 52 pages. Bordeaux: Éditions de l'Attente. ISBN 9782914688666.

Dunn, Jamba (2006). *American Dust*. 123 pages. /ubu editions (Publishing the Unpublishable).

DuPlessis, Rachel Blau (2013-04-15). *Surge: Drafts 96-114*. 184 pages. Cambridge: Salt Publishing. ISBN 9781844719440.

Durbin, Kate (2012). *[PARROT 15] Kept Women*. 16 pages. Los Angeles: Insert Blanc Press. ISSN 2169381115.

Durbin, Kate (2014-05). *E! Entertainment*. 199 pages. Wonder Books. ISBN 9780989598514.

Dutton, Danielle (2007-03-00). *Attempts at a Life*. Grafton: Tarpaulin Sky Press. ISBN 9780977901937.

Dworkin, Craig (2000-02-05). *Smokes*. Poetic Object #3. [Republished in 2004 on /ubu editions.]

Dworkin, Craig (2002). *Index*. Calgary: housepress.

Dworkin, Craig (2003-07-23). *Reading the Illegible*. Evanston:

Northwestern University Press. ISBN 9780810119277.

Dworkin, Craig (2005-11-00). *Strand*. 102 pages. New York: Roof Books. ISBN 9781931824149.

Dworkin, Craig (2006). *Maps*. 7 pages. /ubu editions (Publishing the Unpublishable).

Dworkin, Craig (2006-03-00). *Language to Cover a Page: The Early Writings of Vito Acconci*. 428 pages. Cambridge, MA: The MIT Press. ISBN 9780262012249.

Dworkin, Craig (2008-04-00). *Parse*. 312 pages. Berkeley: Atelos. ISBN 9781891190285.

Dworkin, Craig (2010). *The Perverse Library*. 176 pages. York: information as material. ISBN 9781907468032.

Dworkin, Craig (2011-08). _____. Calgary: No press.

Dworkin, Craig (2015-03-00). *Alkali*. 140 pages. Denver: Counterpath Press. ISBN 9781933996479.

Dworkin, Craig (2016-09-05). *Twelve Erroneous Displacements and a Fact*. 40 pages. York: information as material. ISBN 9781907468247.

Dworkin, Craig, and Goldsmith, Kenneth, eds. (2011-01-00). *Against Expression: An Anthology of Conceptual Writing*. liv; 593

pages. Evanston: Northwestern University Press. ISBN 0810127113.

Earnshaw, Matt (2015-05-04). *INTELLECTUAL PROPERTY SERVICE PLATFORM SUITABLE FOR MODERN SCIENCE AND TECHNOLOGY (MARCH 2015)*. 8 pages. Gauss PDF.

Earnshaw, Matt (2016-03-01). *AGGREGATION, ANALYSIS, AND PRESENTATION OF PORTFOLIO FOR INTELLECTUAL PROPERTY MANAGEMENT (March 2016)*. 8 pages. Gauss PDF.

eckhoff, kevin martins mcpherson (2014). *TITAN*. [36 double pages]. Gauss PDF.

eckhoff, kevin martins mcpherson (2014-09-00). *The Time Machine: Chapter One*. Calgary: Spacecraft Press.

eckhoff, kevin mcpherson (2015-04-00). *Their Biography: an organism of relationships*. 112 pages. Toronto: BookThug. ISBN 9781771660945.

Eisenmann, Jake (2014-03-04). *Unforgeable Poems*. [14/26 blank pages]. Zürich: LUMA Foundation (1000 BOOKS BY 1000 POETS). ISBN 9781304907639.

Elmo, Gum, Heather, Holly, Mistletoe, and Rowan (2002). *Notes Towards the Complete Works of Shakespeare*. 17 pages. vivaria.net. ISBN 095411812X.

Elrick, Laura (2003). *sKincerity*. 82 pages. San Francisco: Krupskaya Books. ISBN 1928650171.

Eric, Caspar, og Karl, Kristian (2014). *Sarah Jessica Parker 2*. 20 pages. Oslo: AFV Press. ISBN 9788293395003.

Erikson, Carl Johan (2013-10-15). *Armageddon – The End, a topographical survey*. 72 pages. Stockholm: OEI editör. ISBN 9789185905539.

Ernst, K.S. (1993). *Moby Dick by Ernest Hemingway*. Press Me Close.

Espinosa, Luis (2011). *Poemas Wiki*. Buenos Aires: Spiral Jetty.

Espitallier, Jean-Michel (2000-01-05). *Gasoil: prises de guerre*. 107 pages. Paris: Flammarion. ISBN 2080679341.

Espitallier, Jean-Michel (2003-03-15). *Le Théorème d'Espitallier*. 139 pages. Paris: Flammarion. ISBN 2080684345.

Estaphin (2008-07-00). *DCLP (District & Central Line Project)*. 176 pages. London: Veer Books. ISBN 9780955876332.

Etherin, Anthony (2015-11-19). *101: A Collection of Palindrome Haiku*. 111 pages. songsofinversion.com.

Etherin, Anthony (2016-04-30). *Micropoetry*. Calgary: Spacecraft Press.

Etherin, Anthony (2016-05). *Anagram-sonnet for Borges*. Calgary: No press.

Etherin, Anthony (2017-01-01). *Fifty Shattered Sculptures: A Miscellany of Experiments Under Constraint*. 21 pages. songsofinversion.com.

Etherin, Anthony (2017-01-15). *FIVE ROMANTICS IN FIRM OCTAVES*. Calgary: No press.

Farrell, Dan (1999). *Last Instance*. 61 pages. San Francisco: Krupskaya Books. ISBN 1928650015.

Farrell, Dan (2000). *The Inkblot Record*. Toronto: Coach House Books. ISBN 9781552450536.

Faylor, J. Gordon (2012). *Docking, Rust Archon*. bass-books. ISBN 9780983762324.

Faylor, J. Gordon (2012-09-29). *MARGINAL CONTRIBUTION TWIN (Title Detail . epub f pdf download add | e t8 pp Lulu 2012 Paperback | rtf · trollthread.tumblr.com 2012 d) [Security | partition http://obesityamerica.bodycleansep roducts.com/ 5.833 8.265 | Lulu Paperback Download; Title Detail . epub f pdf download add | e t8 pp Lulu 2012 Paperback | rtf · trollthread.tumblr.com 2012 d]*. [8; 327 pages]. TROLL THREAD.

Fee, Matthew (2014-02-18). *Genesis // Instructions for Lightning*

Avoidance. [216 pages]. Zürich: LUMA Foundation (1000 BOOKS BY 1000 POETS). ISBN 9781312025806.

Ferguson, Gerald (1978). *The Standard Corpus of Present Day English Language Usage Arranged by Word Length and Alphabetized Within Word Length*. 290 pages. Halifax: NSCAD Press. ISBN 9780919616448. [Second, revised edition according to the NSCAD Press page. National Library of Australia claims to hold an edition dated 1970.]

Ferrari, León (1967). *Palabras Ajenas*. Buenos Aires: Falbo editor.

Figueiredo, César (1998). *24 cartas comerciais tipo*. 60 pages. Porto: Edições Mortas. ISBN 9728313101.

Finch, Andy (2014-11-15). *Sixty Morning Walks*. 184 pages. New York: Ugly Duckling Presse.

Fitch, Andy (2016). *60 Morning Wlaks*. 241 pages. Editions Eclipse.

Fitterman, Robert (2002). *Reading*. Calgary: housepress. ISBN 1894174682.

Fitterman, Robert (2002-05-01). *Metropolis 16-29*. 124 pages. Toronto: Coach House Books. ISBN 9781552451045.

Fitterman, Robert (2004). *This Window Makes Me Feel*. 77 pages. /ubu editions.

Fitterman, Robert (2004-10-01). *Metropolis XXX: The Decline and Fall of the Roman Empire*. 72 pages. Washington, DC: Edge Books. ISBN 9781890311162.

Fitterman, Robert (2006). *HI MY NAME IS*. 20 pages. /ubu editions (Publishing the Unpublishable).

Fitterman, Robert (2008-03-00). *My Sun Also Rises*. Calgary: No press.

Fitterman, Robert (2008-03-00). *The Sun Also Also Rises: A Hemingway Reader*. Calgary: No press.

Fitterman, Robert (2009-03-10). *Rob the Plagiarist*. 107 pages. New York: Roof Books. ISBN 9781931824330.

fitterman, robert (2010). *now we are friends*. 126 pages. Sunnyside, NY: Truck Books. ISBN 9780984885701.

Fitterman, Robert (2010-07-01). *Sprawl*. 81 pages. Los Angeles: Make Now Press. ISBN 9780981596228.

Fitterman, Robert (2011-10-00). *Holocaust Museum*. 124 pages. London: Veer Books. ISBN 9781907088346.

fitterman, robert (2014-03). *JUST ANOTHER SOFT MACHINE*. 34 pages.

London: Veer Books. ISBN 9781907088667.

Fitterman, Robert (2014-03-01). *No, Wait. Yep. Definitely Still Hate Myself.* (illustrated by Natalya Lobanova). 88 pages. New York: Ugly Duckling Presse. ISBN 9781937027322.

Fitterman, Robert (2016-06-01). *Nevermind.* 718 pages. Wonder Books. ISBN 9780989598569.

Fitterman, Robert, and Giasson, Steve (2010-10-00). *Directions.* Calgary: No press.

Fitterman, Robert, and Place, Vanessa (2009-01-01). *Notes on Conceptualisms.* 80 pages. New York: Ugly Duckling Presse. ISBN 9781933254463.

Fitterman, Robert, and Rowntree, Dirk (2006-01-00). *War, the Musical.* 400 pages. Honolulu: subpress collective. ISBN 9781930068339.

Fitzpatrick, Jameson (2014-02-27). *Morrisroe: Erasures.* [60 pages]. Zürich: LUMA Foundation (1000 BOOKS BY 1000 POETS). ISBN 9781312056008.

Ford, G.L. (2008-07-01). *The Invention of Perspective.* 24 pages. New York: Ugly Duckling Presse.

Forman, Alex (2012-04-17). *Tall, Slim & Erect: Portraits of the Presidents*. 131 pages. Los Angeles: Les Figues Press. ISBN 9781934254318.

Forte, Frédéric (2002-07-00). *Discographies*. 124 pages. Bordeaux: Éditions de l'Attente. ISBN 9782914688048.

Forte, Paul (1978). *SYSTEMATICALLY / "SYSTEMATICALLY"*. [20/20 blank pages]. San Francisco: NFS Press; San Jose: Union Gallery.

Forte, Paul (1978). *TITLE*. [20/20 blank pages]. San Francisco: NFS Press; San Jose: Union Gallery.

Foster, Sesshu (2009). *World Ball Notebook*. 138 pages. San Francisco: City Lights Publishers. ISBN 9780872864672.

Fowler, Steven J. (2011). *fights: cycles I-XV*. London: Veer Books. ISBN 9781907088315. [Reissued in (2015-10-00); fights (2nd edition). 124 pages. ISBN 9781907088841.]

Fowler, SJ, & Coyle, Patrick (2011). *Art Gallery Bouncer*. [7 pages]. Gauss PDF.

Fraga, Sophia Le (2013). *I RL, YOU RL*. [72 pages]. minutes BOOKS. [Republished on (2014-09-21). TROLL THREAD.]

Freedman, Lewis, & Rydberg, Kevin (2013-11-16). *SOLITUDE: The Complete Games*. [20 pages]. TROLL THREAD.

Friedlander, Benjamin (2004-04-08). *Simulcast: Four Experiments in Criticism*. 360 pages. Tuscaloosa: University of Alabama Press. ISBN 0817350284.

Friedman, Ed (1979). *The Telephone Book*. 296 pages. New York: Power Mad Press and Telephone Books.

Friedman, Rebecca (2014). *Fro-Yo Diaries*. [14 pages]. Gauss PDF.

Fulton, Colin (2013-09-00). *Life Experience Coolant*. 112 pages. Toronto: BookThug. ISBN 9781927040850.

Funkhouser, Chris (2015-10-12). *Whereis Mineral: Selected Adventures in MOO*. [156 pages]. Gauss PDF Editions.

Furstnau, Timothy (2013-04-05). *How It Hurts*. 82 pages. Portland: Jank Editions/Publication Studio. ISBN 9781624620232.

Gallagher, Kristen (2011). *We Are Here*. 124 pages. Sunnyside, NY: Truck Books. ISBN 9780984885718.

Gallagher, Kristen (2016-04-04). *Grand Central*. [56 pages]. TROLL THREAD.

Gamble, Jay (2015-08-00). *Book of Knots*. 104 pages. Toronto: BookThug. ISBN 9781771661997.

Gangemi, Kenneth (1971). *Lydia*. 77 pages. Los Angeles: Black Sparrow Press. ISBN 9780876850077.

García, Dora (2011). *All the Stories*. 526 pages. London: Book Works/Eastside Projects. ISBN 9781906012366.

Gassilewski, Jörgen (2009-02-26). *Kärleksdikter*. 90 pages. Stockholm: Albert Bonniers Förlag. ISBN 9789100120139.

Gassilewski, Jörgen (2011-11-02). *Hittills samlad poesi 1983-2009*. 852 pages. Stockholm: OEI editör. ISBN 9789185905287.

Gaston, Jesi (2015-03-11). *Crocs' Bible*. [692 pages]. Gauss PDF.

Geffriaud, Mark (2012). *The Curve of Forgotten Things*. 68 pages. London: Book Works. ISBN 9781906012335.

Genschel, Mara (2016-02-17). *Referenzfläche 1#*. edition taberna kritika.

Genusa, Angela (2012-11-25). *The Package Insert of Sorrows*. 45 pages. Lulu.com. ISBN 9781300443940.

Genusa, Angela (2013-01-30). *Tender Buttons*. [40 pages]. Gauss PDF.

Genusa, Angela (2013-08-31). *Highlights For Ren*. 726 pages. Lulu.com. ISBN 9781304193698.

Genusa, Angela (2013-08-31). *onlinedating.teenadultdating / Adult-Dating*. 122 pages. Lulu.com. ISBN 9781300295402.

Genusa, Angela (2013-10-16). *Jane Doe*. [44 pages]. Gauss PDF.

Genusa, Angela (2013-10-19). *Spam Bibliography*. 92 pages. TROLL THREAD.

Genusa, Angela (2013-12-00). *Twentysix Wikipedia Articles*. [461 pages]. Cargo Collective.

Genusa, Angela (2013-12-13). *Musée du Service des Objets Trouvés*. [PediaPress].

Genusa, Angela (2015-02-00). *Simone's Embassy*. 580 pages. Editions Eclipse.

Genusa, Angela (2015-08-24). *TWENTYSIX GASOLINE STATION PRICES*. [28 pages]. Gauss PDF.

Genusa, Angela (2016). *Sure To Come Here Once More: A Performance Of 10 Minutes & 39 Seconds For Cepstral®'s Synthetic Voices*. 22 pages. Evanston: Present Tense Pamphlets.

Genusa, Angela (2016-08-07). \ *OQUE M'RI*. 382 pages. a kind of a huh.

Genusa, Angela (2016-09-09). *V/O*. a kind of a huh.

Genusa, Angela, & Laird, Benjamin (2014-03-30). *Composition*. 625 pages. GPDF Editions.

Ghiu, Bogdan (2006). *(Poemul din carton)*. *Urme de distrugere pe Marte*. 160 pages. București: Cartea Românească. ISBN 9732318902.

Giasson, Steve (2010). ✝ ▐▌. 2636 pages. /ubu editions (Publishing the Unpublishable).

Giasson, Steve (2010). *PSYCHOSIS*. 44 pages. Kingston, PA: Naissance.

Giasson, Steve (2011). *SOME GASOLINE PRICES*. 52 pages. Manchester: Apple Pie Editions.

Giasson, Steve (2011). *Tiffany & Co. Poems*. 280 pages. Manchester: Apple Pie Editions.

Giasson, Steve (2012-05-00). *JE SUIS UN VÉRITABLE ARTISTE*. Calgary: No press.

GIASSON, STEVE (2014-02-03). *AUTOPORTRAIT*. [82/82 blank pages]. TROLL THREAD.

GIASSON, STEVE (2014-02-03). *VIAGGIO IN ITALIA*. [18 pages]. TROLL THREAD.

GIFFIN, LAWRENCE (2011-12-11). *EX TEMPORE*. 176 pages. TROLL THREAD.

GIFFIN, LAWRENCE (2012-12-09). *AD PEDEM LITTERAE*. 3 volumes; 582, 582, 584 pages. TROLL THREAD.

GIFFIN, LAWRENCE (2014-03-02). *QUOD VIDE*. 102 pages. TROLL THREAD.

GIFFIN, LAWRENCE (2014-03-02). *NON FACIT SALTUS*. 102 pages. TROLL THREAD.

Giffin, Lawrence (2015). *white future*. 190 pages. orworse press.

Gilbert, Annette, ed. (2014). *Reprint. Appropriation (&) Literature*. 580 pages. Wiesbaden: Luxbooks. ISBN 9783939557678.

Gilet, Margaux (2014-11-07). *Images*. [22/22 blank pages]. Zürich: LUMA Foundation (1000 BOOKS BY 1000 POETS). ISBN 9781312661851.

Gillespie, Abraham Lincoln (1980). *The Syntactic Revolution*. (Milazzo, Richard, ed.) New York: Out Of London Press. ISBN 091557005X.

Gilsdorf, Dan (2014). *Repo Man*. 139 pages. Portland: Jank Editions/Publication Studio. ISBN 9781624620454.

Gins, Madeline (1984). *What The President Will Say and Do!!*. 149 pages. Barrytown: Station Hill Press. ISBN 9780930794927.

Gins, Madeleine and Arakawa (2006-11-00). *Making Dying Illegal*. 224 pages. New York: Roof Books. ISBN 9781931824224.

Giovenale, Marco (2014-09-00). *white while*. [20 pages]. Gauss PDF.

Giraudon, Liliane (2012-06-15). *Les Pénétrables*. 336 pages. Paris: Éditions P.O.L. ISBN 9782818016480.

Gizzi, Peter (2012-12-31). *Ode: Salute to the New York School, 1950-1970 (A Libretto)*. 64 pages. Tucson: Letter Machine Editions. ISBN 9780981522777.

Gladman, Renee (2003-08-15). *The Activist*. 145 pages. San Francisco: Krupskaya Books. ISBN 192865018x.

Goldman, Judith (2006). *DeathStar/rico-chet*. 120 pages. Oakland, CA: O Books. ISBN 9781882022618.

Goldman, Judith (2001). *Vocoder*. 93 pages. New York: Roof Books. ISBN 9780937804896.

Goldsmith, Kenneth (1994). *No. 109 2.7.93-12.15.93*. [16 pages]. New York: Editions Bravin Post Lee.

Goldsmith, Kenneth (1997). *No. 111 2.7.93-10.20.96*. 606 pages. Great Barrington: The Figures. ISBN 0935724877.

Goldsmith, Kenneth (1998-01-14). *Fidget*. 112 pages. Toronto: Coach House Books. ISBN 9781552450765.

Goldsmith, Kenneth (1999). *Gertrude Stein on Punctuation*. Newton: Abaton Books.

Goldsmith, Kenneth (2000). *6799*. 92 pages. zingmagazine.

Goldsmith, Kenneth (2001). *Soliloquy*. 489 pages. New York: Granary Books. ISBN 9781887123532.

Goldsmith, Kenneth (2001-02-12). *Cigna*. Calgary: housepress.

Goldsmith, Kenneth (2002). *Head Citations*. 88 pages. Great Barrington: The Figures. ISBN 9781930589155.

Goldsmith, Kenneth (2003). *Day*. 836 pages. Great Barrington: The Figures. ISBN 9781930589209. [Previously published as excerpt; (2001-02-12). Calgary: housepress.]

Goldsmith, Kenneth (2005). *The Weather*. 120 pages. Los Angeles: Make Now Press. ISBN 9780974355429.

Goldsmith, Kenneth (2007). *Traffic*. 115 pages. Los Angeles: Make Now Press. ISBN 9780974355481.

Goldsmith, Kenneth (2008). *All The Numbers From Numbers*. 21 pages. /ubu editions (Publishing the Unpublishable).

Goldsmith, Kenneth (2008). *SPORTS*. 122 pages. Los Angeles: Make Now Press. ISBN 9780974355498.

Goldsmith, Kenneth (2011-09-20). *Uncreative Writing*. 272 pages. New

York: Columbia University Press. ISBN 9780231149914.

Goldsmith, Kenneth (2013-03-00). *Seven American Deaths and Disasters*. 176 pages. New York: powerHouse Books. ISBN 9781576876367.

Goldsmith, Kenneth (2013-07-00). *Being Dumb*. Calgary: No press.

"Goldsmith, Kenneth" (2014-05-26). *Autobiography*. Lulu.com. ISBN 9781312225480.

Goldsmith, Kenneth (2015-11-00). *Capital: New York, Capital of the 20th Century*. 928 pages. Verso Books. ISBN 9781784781569.

Goma, Paul (2004). *Alfabecedar - cuvântar -*. 337 pages. Bucureşti: Editura Victor Frunză. ISBN 9739120423. [Digital edition out in 2009; 764 pages. 1st edition was self-released in 4 typewritten volumes, 1981.]

gomringer, eugen (2002). *grammatische konfession*. 188 pages. Paris: onestar press.

Gonzales-Foerster, Dominique (2014-03-13). *1887 - Splendide Hotel*. 126 pages. Paris: onestar press. [2nd edition.]

González, Alberto Sesmero (2014-09-23). *©ircunstancias*. [53 pages]. Zürich: LUMA Foundation (1000

BOOKS BY 1000 POETS). ISBN 9781312547094.

Goodland, Gilles (2006-09-15). *Capital*. 123 pages. Cambridge: Salt Publishing. ISBN 9781844712632.

Gordon, Nada (2007-04-01). *Folly*. 121 pages. New York: Roof Books. ISBN 9781931824231.

Gordon, Noah Eli (2006-11-00). *Inbox*. 79 pages. Buffalo: BlazeVOX [books]. ISBN 1934289205.

Goring, Nals, & Phillips, Zach (2015-03-10). *Chomo Analects*. [474 pages]. Gauss PDF.

Gottlieb, Michael (2003-03-00). *Lost and Found*. 80 pages. New York: Roof Books. ISBN 9781931824088.

Gower, Terence, and Torre, Mónica de la (1999-10-02). *Appendices, Illustrations & Notes*. 64 pages. Culver City: Smart Art Press. ISBN 1889195359.

Graff, Rasmus (2008-08-06). *patchwork*. 16 pages. København: Forlaget 28/6. ISBN 9788799268610.

Graff, Rasmus (2009-03-17). *Som levende begravet her*. 24 pages. København: Forlaget 28/6. ISBN 9788799268696.

Graff, Rasmus (2010-07-00). *FOLKETS PROSA*. 126 pages. Århus: Edition After Hand. ISBN 9788787489669.

Graff, Rasmus (2014-11-00). *Lavet efter Kina*. 48 pages. Århus: Antipyrine. ISBN 9788793108196.

Graff, Rasmus, Kristensen, Sigurd Buch og Møller, Martin Johs. (2008-08-03). *De helvedes lambier ødelægger mine sandheder*. 80 pages. København: Forlaget 28/6. ISBN 9788799268603.

Graham, Dan (2009-06-30). *Dan Graham: Works, and Collected Writings; Text by Gloria Moure*. 295 pages. Barcelona: Ediciones Polígrafa S.A. ISBN 9788434312012.

Grangaud, Michelle (1997-04-00). *Poèmes fondus*. 128 pages. Paris: P.O.L. éditeur. ISBN 2867445566.

Grangaud, Michelle (2001-05-00). *Calendrier des poètes. L'année folle 1*. 192 pages. Paris: P.O.L. éditeur. ISBN 2867448344.

Grangaud, Michelle (2003-02-00). *Calendrier des fêtes nationales. L'année folle II*. 256 pages. Paris: P.O.L éditeur. ISBN 2867449316.

Gray, Anna, & Paulsen, Ryan Wilson (2009). *One-Way Street: An Index*. 53 pages. [/ubu editions (Publishing the Unpublishable)].

Green, Faye (2014-02-16). *NOT TO DISCOU[RAGE] YOU*. [58 pages]. Zürich: LUMA Foundation (1000

BOOKS BY 1000 POETS). ISBN 9781312021150.

Greene, Virginie (2011-11-00). *Cent vues de John Harvard*. 112 pages. Bordeaux: Éditions de l'Attente. ISBN 9782362420160.

Griffin, Jeff (2013-10-15). *Lost And*. 170 pages. Iowa City: University of Iowa Press (Kuhl House Poets). ISBN 9781609381998.

groh, benjamin (2016-12-18). *passagenarbeit*. Calgary: No press.

gross, lukas (2008-01-22). *glatteis - neue meister*. 226 pages. TRAUMAWIEN.

Gudding, Gabriel (2015-11-00). *Literature for Nonhumans*. 144 pages. Boise: Ahsahta Press. ISBN 9781934103630.

Gumz, Alexander (2015). *verschwörungscartoons [New York Flarf Gedichte]*. Köln: parasitenpresse.

Gumz, Alexander, Porombka, Stephan, und Töpfer, Andreas (2012). *Flarf: 95 Netzgedichte*. 128 pages. Hildesheim: Verlag Edition Pæchterhaus. ISBN 9783941392328.

Hajnoczky, Helen (2011-03-00). *Viau's Corsets*. Calgary: No press.

Hale, Joe (2014). *Getting Inside Simon Morris' Head*. 324 pages. York: information as material. ISBN 9781907468216.

Hall, Lyndl (2012). *Latitudes and Longitudes of the Principal Ports, Harbours, Headlands, etc., in the World*. 86 pages. Vancouver: Bookmachine/Publication Studio. ISBN 9781927385036.

Hallberg, Anna (2010-08-00). *Colosseum, Kolosseum*. 160 pages. Stockholm: Albert Bonniers Förlag. ISBN 9789100124533.

Hamilton, Diana (2012-10-06). *Okay, Okay*. 73 pages. Sunnyside, NY: Truck Books. ISBN 9780984885732.

Hampshire, Alex (2015-09-08). *ENERGY & PRIVACY*. [38 pages]. Gauss PDF.

Hansen-Fliedner, Dylan (2012-11-29). *correspondence*. 266 pages. Lulu.com. ISBN 9781300459415.

Hansen-Fliedner, Dylan (2013-12-13). *Linger in Heat*. 59 pages. d^a^t^a press. ISBN 9781304712578.

Hansen-Fliedner, Dylan (2014). *Team Hansen*. [38 pages]. Gauss PDF.

Hansen-Fliedner, Dylan (2014-02-15). *HARD HELL*. [254 pages]. Zürich: LUMA Foundation (1000 BOOKS BY 1000 POETS). ISBN 9781312017467.

Hansen-Fliedner, Dylan, and Jadick, Jay (2013-12-17). *P(auto)COET*. 89 pages. d^a^t^a press. ISBN 9781304724403.

Hansen-Fliedner, Dylan,/Schimmel, Seth (2015-01-25). *TEH/THE?*. [2 volumes; 501 pages each]. GPDF Editions.

Hanitzsch, Eugênia Pessoa (2015-02-17). *Visual Diary*. [54 pages]. Zürich: LUMA Foundation (1000 BOOKS BY 1000 POETS). ISBN 9781312927230.

Harris, Jesse (2013-06-00). *Pop Art Poem (with Advertising)*. [34 pages]. Guelph: Publication Studio. ISBN 9780992036614.

Harvey, Michael (1971). *White Papers 1968-1971*. [71 cards].

Hatherly, Ana (2001). *Um calculador de improbabilidades*. 79 pages. Lisboa: Quimera. ISBN 9725890590.

Haven, Leif (2014-10-11). *The Joy of Pain*. 20 pages. San Francisco: Solar ▲ Luxuriance.

Hawkey, Christian (2010-10-25). *Ventrakl*. 152 pages. New York: Ugly Duckling Presse. ISBN 9781933254647.

Heidsieck, Bernard (1998). *Vaduz*. [40 pages + CD]. Venezia: Archivio F. Conz Associazione Culturale.

Heidsieck, Bernard (2013-09-00). *Tapuscrits — Poèmes-Partitions, Biopsies, Passe-Partout*. 1184 pages. Dijon: Les presses du réel. ISBN 9782840665151.

Heisler, Yasmin (2016-08). *Aquarium Drift*. [16 double pages]. SOd press.

Heldén, Johannes, & Jonson, Håkan (2014-05-17). *Evolution*. 240 pages. Stockholm: OEI editör. ISBN 9789185905669.

Helsem, Michael (1982). *carnivorous equations 2*. West Lima: Xerox Sutra Editions.

Higgins, Dick (1969). *foew&ombwhnw: a grammar of the mind and a phenomenology of love and a science of the arts as seen by a stalker of the wild mushroom*. 320 pages. New York: Something Else Press.

Higgins, Dick (1974-12-00). *Modular Poems*. 158 pages. Barton: Unpublished Editions. ISBN 9780914162056.

Hilder, Jamie (2011). *Affidavit*. 68 pages. Vancouver: Bookmachine / Publication Studio. ISBN 9781935662204.

Hix, H.L. (2007-10-01). *God Bless*. 174 pages. Wilkes-Barre: Etruscan Press. ISBN 9780974599571.

hjort, jan (2009-03-02). *nipsonanomimatamimonanopsin; collager af Viggo Madsen*. 40 pages. København: Forlaget 28/6. ISBN 9788799268665.

Hobogrammathon, Toadex (2004). *Name, A Novel*. 137 pages. /ubu editions.

Hofer, Jen, and Magi, Jill (2013). *Shroud: A Piece of Fabric Sewn To A Piece of Paper By Way of A Map.*

Hoff, James (2014-04-09). *Every Second One Hundred Bolts of Lightning Strike the Earth.* 80 pages. Vancouver: Bookmachine/Publication Studio. ISBN 9781927385135.

Hoffmann, Cheryl (2014-02-11). *The Currant.* [63 pages]. Zürich: LUMA Foundation (1000 BOOKS BY 1000 POETS). ISBN 9781312006621.

Holmqvist, Karl (2009). *What's My Name?.* 128 pages. London: Book Works. ISBN 9781906012182.

Holson, Dennis (2016-02-05). *Um Bla.* Calgary: Spacecraft Press.

Hoover, Paul (2009-11-01). *Sonnet 56.* 81 pages. Los Angeles: Les Figues Press. ISBN 9781934254127.

HOPELY, EDDIE (2013-09-11). *SNUG.* [48 pages]. TROLL THREAD.

Hou Je Bek, Wilfried (2008). *Gilgamesh for Apes.*

Howe, Susan (1989-12-00). *A Bibliography of the King's Book; or, Eikon Basilike.* 64 pages. Providence: Paradigm Press. ISBN 0945926138.

Howe, Susan (1993-06-17). *The Nonconformist's Memorial: Poems by...* 160 pages. New York: New Directions. ISBN 9780811212298.

Howe, Susan (2010-12-31). *That This*. 112 pages. New York: New Directions. ISBN 9780811219181.

Howse, Martin (2013). *Diff in June*. 740 pages. Brescia: LINK Editions. ISBN 9781291503593.

Högström, Martin (2007-06-00). *Kommande industrilandskap*. 98 pages. Stockholm: OEI editör. ISBN 9789197601474.

Huang, Yunte (2004). *Cribs*. 59 pages. Kaneohe: Tinfish Press. ISBN 0975937618.

Huebler, Douglas (2002). *Secrets (Variable Piece 4, New York City)*. 124 pages. /ubu editions.

Hunt, Ken (2014-02-00). *Top Secret Calligraphy*. Calgary: No press.

Hunt, Ken (2014-02-11). *Space Administration*. 146 pages. Zürich: LUMA Foundation (1000 BOOKS BY 1000 POETS). ISBN 9781312006515. [Special edition: (2014-06-13). Calgary: Spacecraft Press.].

Hunt, Ken (2014-06-05). *Daisy Knell*. Calgary: No press.

Hunt, Ken (2014-12-00). *The Passage Lies Here*. Calgary: No press.

Hunt, Ken (2015-01-28). *CONFIDENTIAL*. Calgary: Spacecraft Press.

Hunt, Ken (2015-02-01). *Three translations of Haiku by a Robot by Nathan Beifuss*. Calgary: Spacecraft Press.

Hunt, Ken (2016-03-00). *Antiverse Palindrome*. Calgary: No press.

Hunt, Ken (2016-04-30). *HALPHABET*. Calgary: Spacecraft Press.

Hurtado, Amanda (2014). *S A CE P*. [127 double pages]. Editions Eclipse.

Huot, Claire, and Majzels, Robert (2013-09-18). *85*. 5 volumes. Los Angeles: Les Figues Press. ISBN 9781934254417.

Hüls, Maximiliane (2013). *Das Buch Stéphane Mallarmés*. 328 pages.

"INTERN" (2015-09-13). *INTERN*. [304 pages]. TROLL THREAD.

Islam, Austin (2015-02-16). *watching fox news on mute: a collection of facebook statuses from march 5, 2014 to july 5, 2012*. [104 pages]. Zürich: LUMA Foundation (1000 BOOKS BY 1000 POETS). ISBN 9781312924093.

Jacobs, Sarah (2007). *Deciphering Human Chromosome 16: Index to the Report*. 552 pages. York: information as material. ISBN 9780955309229.

Jacquet, Élisabeth (2006-03-00). *Le supplément télévision*. 52 pages. Bordeaux: Éditions de l'Attente. ISBN 9782914688444.

Jadick, Jason (2012-12-14). *The Uncreative Subterranean*. 153 pages. Lulu.com. ISBN 9781300525981.

Jadick, Jay (2014-02-18). *ed/it/ed*. [304 pages]. Zürich: LUMA Foundation (1000 BOOKS BY 1000 POETS). ISBN 9781312026766.

Jaeger, Peter (2009-05-12). *Rapid Eye Movement*. 156 pages. London: Reality Street. ISBN 9781874400417.

Jaeger, Peter (2011). *The Persons*. 54 pages. York: information as material. ISBN 9781907468049.

Jaeger, Peter (2013-04-24). *A Field Guide for Silas*. Calgary: No press.

Jaeger, Peter (2015-01-00). *Co-ordinates (for Theodor Herzl)*. Calgary: No press.

Jaubert, Aurélia (2014). *Une capture de caractères*. 14 pages. Clamart: Les Cahiers de la Seine.

Jelen, Isabelle (2002-08-00). *Collection particulière*. 36 pages. Bordeaux: Éditions de l'Attente. ISBN 9782914688086.

Jelen, Isabelle (2004-10-00). *Marche Mars*. Bordeaux: Éditions de l'Attente. ISBN 9782914688277.

Johnson, Kent (2008). *Poetic Architecture*. 48 pages. Kenmore:

BlazeVOX [books]. ISBN 9781934289327.

Johnson, Kent (2010). *Day*. The Figures; BlazeVOX [books]. ISBN 9781935402992.

JOHNSON, MARK (2015-10-07). *YELLOW HIGHLIGHTER*. [52 pages]. TROLL THREAD.

Jones, Clara B. (2016-04-28). *Autopsy: Exploratory Poems*. 32 pages. GPDF Editions.

Jones, Doug (2013-03-00). *Posts*. London: Veer Books. ISBN 9781907088506.

Jones, Russel (2015-09-03). *Birds 1.0*. Calgary: Spacecraft Press.

Jordheim, Cecilie Bjørgås (2015-07-00). *The Great Treatise*. Calgary: No press.

Joseph, Manuel (2010-05-00). *La Tête au carré*. 72 pages. Paris: Éditions P.O.L. ISBN 9782818012468.

Joyce, James (2013-09-00). *Giacomo Joyce mit zwei Aneignungen ins Deutsche von Alban Nikolai Herbst und Helmut Schulze*. 72 pages. Bern: edition taberna kritika. ISBN 9783905846256.

Kake, yks (2012-06-12). *Pääteokseni I--III*. 82 pages. Helsinki: ntamo. ISBN 9789522151872.

Kamerman, Richard (2011). *I Stayed In The Apartment For Thirty Two*

Days Without Leaving. [28314 pages]. Gauss PDF.

Kapil, Bhanu (2001-10-12). *The Vertical Interrogation of Strangers*. Berkeley: Kelsey Street Press. ISBN 0932716563.

Kapil, Bhanu (2006-08-00). *Incubation: a space for monsters*. 95 pages. New York: Leon Works. ISBN 9780976582021.

Kaplan, Josef (2012). *Boner Transcript*. [16 pages]. calmaplombprombombbalm.com.

Kaplan, Josef (2012). *Democracy is not for the People*. 102 pages. Sunnyside, NY: Truck Books. ISBN 9780984885749.

KAPLAN, JOSEF (2012-03-21). *1-100*. [16 volumes; 234 pages each]. TROLL THREAD.

KAPLAN, JOSEF (2013-10-12). *Kill List*. 68 pages. Baltimore: CARS ARE REAL. ISBN 9780989803311.

Karmin, Jennifer (2016). *art is a concept art is a process*. [4 pages]. Evanston: Present Tense Pamphlets.

Katchadjian, Pablo (2007). *El Martín Fierro ordenado alfabéticamente*. Buenos Aires: Imprenta Argentina de Poesía. ISBN 9872263647.

Katchadjian, Pablo (2009). *El Aleph engordado*. 50 pages. Buenos Aires: Imprenta Argentina de Poesía.

Katchadjian, Pablo (2011). *Mucho trabajo*. Buenos Aires: Spiral Jetty.

Katko, Justin (2011-12-00). *The Death of Pringle*. 100 pages. London: Veer Books. ISBN 9781907088131.

Katz, Vincent (2008). *Shopping for Oliver's Chili*. 3 pages. /ubu editions (Publishing the Unpublishable).

Kaufman, Andrew (2011). *Selected Business Correspondence*. 108 pages. Toronto: The Book Bakery/Publication Studio. ISBN 9780986908910.

Kay, Emma (1999-06-30). *Worldview*. 224 pages. London: Book Works. ISBN 9781870699372.

Kearney, Douglas (2009-11-00). *The Black Automaton*. 95 pages. New York: Fence Books. ISBN 9781934200285.

Keller, Jean (2011-02-07). *The Overlook Manuscript*. 120 pages. Blurb.

Kennedy, Bill, and Wershler-Henry, Darren (2006-04-01). *Apostrophe*. 296 pages. Toronto: ECW Press. ISBN 9781550227222.

Kennedy, Bill, and Wershler-Henry, Darren (2010-10-10). *Update*. 79 pages. Montreal: Snare Books. ISBN 9780981248868.

killian, kevin (2006-08). *Selected Amazon Reviews*; edited by brent cunningham. 54 pages. oakland: hooke press.

killian, kevin (2011-05-00). *Selected Amazon Reviews: Volume Two*. Push Press.

Kim, Sydney S. (2012-10-26). *Lessons From A Lonely Italian*. 131 pages. Portland: Jank Editions/Publication Studio. ISBN 9781935662914.

Kirby, Michael (2016-04-06). *GLOSSARY*. [13 pages]. Gauss PDF.

Kivland, Sharon (2006). *Freud on Holiday Volume I: Freud Dreams of Rome*. 32 pages. York: information as material. ISBN 9780955309205.

Kivland, Sharon (2008). *Freud on Holiday Volume II: A Disturbance of Memory*. 186 pages. Athens: Cubearteditions; York: information as material. ISBN 9780955309236.

Kivland, Sharon (2010). *Reisen I*. 16 pages. York: information as material. ISBN 9781907468018.

Kivland, Sharon (2011). *Reisen II*. 20 pages. York: information as material. ISBN 97819074680701.

Kivland, Sharon (2013). *Freud on Holiday: Appendices I-IV*. 4 volumes; 20 pages each. York: information as material. ISBN 9781907468162.

Klauke, Michael (1987). *ad infinitum*. [64 pages]. Atlanta: Nexus Press.

KLOTZMAN, LAUREN (2015-05-11). *MEAT JOY ERROR FAILURE*. [8 volumes; cca. 694 pages each].TROLL THREAD.

Knowles, Alison (1969). *House of Dust*. Cologne: Verlag Gebr. König.

Knowles, Alison (2011). *Clear Skies All Week*. 64 pages. Paris: onestar press.

Knowles, Alison, Schmit, Tomas, Patterson, Benjamin, and Corner, Philip (1965). *The Four Suits*. 192 pages. New York: Something Else Press.

Knowles, Christopher (1979). *Typings (1974-1977)*. [110 pages]. New York: Vehicle Editions. ISBN 093142836X.

Knowles, David (2013). *ISBN: 978-1-62462-012-6*. Variable size. Portland: Jank Editions/Publication Studio. ISBN 9781624620126.

Kodal, Janus (2008-12-28). *Tokyo*. 20 pages. København: Forlaget 28/6. ISBN 9788799268641.

Koeneke, Rodney (2010-12-00). *Names of the Hits (of Diane Warren)*. OMG! Press.

Kokko, Karri (2007). *Avokyyhky, lattiaheroiini*. 91 pages.

Helsinki: ntamo.   ISBN
9789522150288.

Kokko,   Karri   (2016-02-00).
Retweeted. 560 pages. Helsinki:
ntamo. ISBN 9789522156266.

Kolewe,   R.   (2014-09-00).
Afterletters. 64 pages. Toronto:
BookThug. ISBN 9781771660549.

KOPEL, DANA (2015-02-17).   *P(UR)E
IM(MAN)ENCE*. [40 pages]. Zürich:
LUMA Foundation (1000 BOOKS BY
1000 POETS). ISBN 9781312927674.
[Previously published digitally on
Gauss PDF.

Kostelanetz,   Richard   (1979).
Exhaustive Parallel Intervals. 275
pages. New York: Future Press.
ISBN 9780918406095.

Kostelanetz,   Richard   (1982).
Arenas/Fields/Pitches/Turfs.   70
pages. Kansas City: BkMk Press
Books. ISBN 9780933532427.

Kosuth, Joseph (2000). *Purloined: A
Novel*. Cologne: Salon Verlag. 120
pages. ISBN 9783897700154.

KOTECHA, SHIV (2011-12-01).   *PAINT
THE ROCK*. [124 pages].   TROLL
THREAD.

KOTECHA, SHIV (2012-07-13). *OUTFITS*.
[184 pages]. TROLL THREAD.

Kotecha,   Shiv   (2015-08-28).
EXTRIGUE. 98 pages. Los Angeles:
Make   Now   Press.   ISBN
9781942272021.

Kotecha, Shiv (2016). *HOW YOU REMEMBER THE IRON HORSE OR "THE IRON HORSE"*. [16 pages]. Evanston: Present Tense Pamphlets.

Kubíček, Jan [Lakatoš, Klement Václav] (2012). *Kapitalistické básně*. Praha: Petr Štengl. ISBN 9788087563052.

Kuenstler, Frank (1964). *LENS*. 91 pages. [New York]: Film Culture/Harry Gantt.

Kuenstler, Frank (1966). *Fugitives. Rounds*. [130 pages]. New York: Eventorium Press.

Kunin, Aaron (2004). *The Mauberley Series*. 30 pages. /ubu editions.

Kunin, Aaron (2009). *Cold Genius*. 26 pages. The Phsyiocrats. [Larger edition published in (2014-12-02); 80 pages. New York: Fence Books. ISBN 9781934200841.]

Kunin, Aaron (2010-04-01). *The Sore Throat & Other Poems*. 125 pages. New York: Fence Books. ISBN 9781934200346.

Larkin, Maryrose (2009). *DARC*. FLASH+CARD.

Lawson, Gil (2014-03-19). *AR STRATEGY GUIDE*. [68 pages]. Zürich: LUMA Foundation (1000 BOOKS BY 1000 POETS). ISBN 9781304954121.

Lax, Robert (2013-11-00). *Poems (1962-1997)*, edited by John Beer.

400 pages. Seattle: Wave Books. ISBN 9781933517766.

leac, v. (2013-06-21). *unchiul este încântat*. 94 pages. Bistriţa: Editura Charmides. ISBN 9789737659934.

Leach, Mark (2008-07-08). *Marienbad My Love*. 10710 pages. Texas UFO Network.

Leach, Mark (2011-03-12). *#EMPiREFiLM*. 90 pages. CreateSpace Independent Publishing Platform. ISBN 9781460981320.

Leach, Mark (2011-04-24). *Cutting Up Two Burroughs*. 126 pages. CreateSpace Independent Publishing Platform. ISBN 9781461041702.

Leach, Mark (2011-04-29). *Nobody's Coming Back To Uranus: A sci-fi reboot of "Traffic," Kenneth Goldsmith's appropriation of New York City radio reports*. 112 pages. CreateSpace Independent Publishing Platform. ISBN 9781461121213.

Leach, Mark (2011-05-15). *Give Me A VERB 51: An Epic Poem Of The Apollo 11 Moon Landing*. 118 pages. CreateSpace Independent Publishing Platform. ISBN 9781461192046.

Leach, Mark (2011-07-18). *Shoplifting From Uranus*. 140 pages. CreateSpace Independent

Publishing Platform. ISBN 9781463735234.

Leach, Mark (2011-08-01). *I'll Be Your Warhol*. 148 pages. CreateSpace Independent Publishing Platform. ISBN 9781463782610.

Leach, Mark (2011-08-01). *Writing Through John Cage*. 190 pages. CreateSpace Independent Publishing Platform. ISBN 9781463781262.

Leach, Mark (2011-09-14). *31 Days, 31 Novels*. 242 pages. CreateSpace Independent Publishing Platform. ISBN 9781466304741.

Leach, Mark (2011-12-31). *Paragraphs On Postconceptual Writing: A Novel*. 140 pages. CreateSpace Independent Publishing Platform. ISBN 9781468155150.

Leach, Mark (2013-03-23). *SCUW Womanifesto*. 34 pages. Lulu.com. ISBN 9781300868699.

Leeville, Leevistä (ed.). *LEHTOlapset*. 64 pages. Helsinki: ntamo. ISBN 9789522151568.

Lefebvre, Henri (2004-11-08). *les unités perdues*. Paris: Virgile. ISBN 9782914481311.

Lefebvre, Henri (2013-06-00). *Les Restes, prototype*. 52 pages. Paris: Manuella éditions. ISBN 9782917217351.

Lee, Joyce S. (2016-01-17). *Defying Gravity*. [59 pages]. Gauss PDF Editions.

Lee, Sang Woo (2014-02-19). 7 *Poems - Line 2 Project,* 7편의 시- 2호선 프로젝트. [70 pages]. Zürich: LUMA Foundation (1000 BOOKS BY 1000 POETS). ISBN 9781312031128.

Lehto, Leevi (2004). *Ampauksia ympäripyörivästä raketista.* 64 pages. Turku: Savukeidas Kustannus. ISBN 95255000505.

Lehto, Leevi (2012). *Päivä.* 233 pages. Helsinki: ntamo. ISBN 9789522152619.

Leibovici, Franck (2009). *9+11 [2005].* [136 pages]. [/ubu editions (Publishing the Unpublishable)].

León, Oliver (2014-03-17). *Primer cuaderno.* [62 pages]. Zürich: LUMA Foundation (1000 BOOKS BY 1000 POETS). ISBN 9781304947093.

Leshner, Sasha (2015-02-03). *OK, CUPID.* [54 pages]. Zürich: LUMA Foundation (1000 BOOKS BY 1000 POETS). ISBN 9781312891494.

Leslie, Woody (2015-10-01). *Courier's Text Atlas of The United States of America.* New York: Ugly Duckling Presse.

Lespiau, David (2005-05-00). *La poule est un oiseau autodidacte.*

66 pages. Bordeaux: Éditions de l'Attente. ISBN 9782914688369.

Lespiau, David (2008). *Ouija Board*, avec traductions de Cole Swensen et Cosima Weiter. 96 pages. Genève: Héros-Limite. ISBN 9782940358151.

Licht, Alan (2008). *Spring Without Alan Licht / Dime Double Minutemen Nickels On The / Lou Reed Minus Lou Reed / (Give Them Enough Nope)*. 19 pages. /ubu editions (Publishing the Unpublishable).

Lin, Tan (2003). *BlipSoak01*. 336 pages. Berkeley: Atelos. ISBN 1891190180.

lin, tan (2007). *ambience is a novel with a logo*. [28 pages]. Cambridge, MA: katalanché press.

Lin, Tan (2007). *BIB*. 268 pages. /ubu editions (Publishing the Unpublishable).

Lin, Tan (2009-01-05). *HEATH: plagiarism/outsource*. [86 pages]. Tenerife: Zasterle Press. [2nd, revised edition: (2011-12-15). HEATH COURSE PAK. Denver: Counterpath Press. ISBN 9781933996271.]

Lin, Tan (2010-03-00). *Seven Controlled Vocabularies and Obituary 2004, the Joy of Cooking [AIRPORT NOVEL MUSICAL POEM PAINTING FILM PHOTO HALLUCINATION*

LANDSCAPE]. 224 pages. Middletown: Wesleyan University Press. ISBN 9780819569295.

Lin, Tan (2011). *Insomnia and the Aunt*. Chicago: Kenning Editions. ISBN 9780976736479.

LINDER, ISAAC (2012-03-03). *THE MOVIEGOER*. 332 pages. TROLL THREAD.

lloyd, chris (2011-04-10). *Dear PM: letters from the campaign*. 133 pages. [Lulu].

Lomax, Dana Teen (2011-12-00). *Disclosure*. 81 pages. Black Radish Books. ISBN 9780982573174.

Longman, Madelaine Caritas (2015-09-03). *Terms and Conditions for Non-Human Visitors*. Calgary: Spacecraft Press.

lopes, damian (2016-04-00). *en vers un beau lieu: beaulieu inverse*. Calgary: No press.

Lorange, Astrid (2013). *FOOD TURNS INTO BLOOD*. 60 pages. GPDF Editions.

Low, Trisha (2010). *Confessions [of a variety.]*. [19 pages]. Gauss PDF.

Low, Trisha (2012-09-01). *PURGE: Vol. 1: The Last Will & Testament of Trisha Low*. 124 pages. TROLL THREAD.

Low, Trisha (2013). *THE COMPLEAT PURGE*. Chicago: Kenning Editions. ISBN 9780984647552.

Low, Trisha, & Antoine, Tyler (2011). *TARGET IS BUSTLING AND FRIENDLY*. 26 pages. Gauss PDF.

Lucas, Kristin (2013-05-16). *DOLLAR STORE QUALITY PIECE OF SCRAP*. [16 pages]. Brooklyn, NY: Eyebeam; Portland: Jank Editions/Publication Studio. ISBN 9781624620294.

Mabb, Oren (2014-10-17). *Double Address to Hoof Sedition College Graduating Caste of 2091*. [46 pages]. Zürich: LUMA Foundation (1000 BOOKS BY 1000 POETS). ISBN 9781312606357.

Mac Cormack, Karen (2008-08-15). *Implexures (complete edition)*. 125 pages. Tucson: Chax Press. ISBN 9780925904744.

Macdonald, Travis (2015-04-08). *3 Selections from '.3...'*. Calgary: Spacecraft Press.

Mac Low, Jackson (1989-04-28). *Words nd Ends from Ez*. 93 pages. Bolinas: Avenue B. ISBN 9780939691036.

Mac Low, Jackson (2007-12-00). *The Twin Plays: Port-au-Prince & Adams County Illinois*. 16 pages. New York: A Great Bear Pamphlet/Primary Information.

Maguire, Shannon (2013-05-00). *fur(l) parachute*. 112 pages. Toronto: BookThug. ISBN 9781927040607.

Malla, Pasha (2011). *Why We Fight > Quran Neck*. 100 pages. Toronto: The Book Bakery/Publication Studio. ISBN 9780986908903.

Mainella, Dane (2014-02-27). *NOTES*. [636 pages]. Zürich: LUMA Foundation (1000 BOOKS BY 1000 POETS). ISBN 9781312055971.

Mancini, Donato (2005-10-06). *Ligatures*. 112 pages. Vancouver: New Star Books. ISBN 9781554200177.

Manson, Peter (2004). *Adjunct: An Undigest*. 87 pages. Edinburgh: Edinburgh Review. ISBN 9781859332221.

Manson, Peter (2006). *English in Mallarmé*. 87 pages. /ubu editions (Publishing the Unpublishable).

Maranda, Michael [as Marcel Proust] (2006-10-10). *All The Names of "In Search of Lost Time"*. 2 vol.; 568 pages each. Parasitic Ventures Press. ISBN 0969736843.

Marshall, Ian (2009). *Walden By Haiku*. 270 pages. Athens, GA: University of Georgia Press. ISBN 9780820336152.

Matchak, Marc (2014-09-11). *Name Economie*. [56 pages]. Gauss PDF.

Mathews, Harry (1988-01-01). *20 Lines a Day*. 134 pages. Champaign: Dalkey Archive Press. ISBN 9781564781680.

Martínez, Juan Luis (1977). *La nueva novela*. 152 pages. Santiago de Chile: Ediciones Archivo.

Martrich, Andy (2014-02-00). *NJN Transition*. [104 pages]. Gauss PDF.

Martrich, Andy (2015-03-01). *Blackmar-Diemer Gambit*. [27 pages]. GPDF Editions.

Martrich, Andy (2016). *Pitching with Demonic Sigil Grips*. [40 pages]. Los Angeles: PRB Editions.

Maxwell, Andrew (2014-12-15). *Candor is the brightest shield*. 208 pages. New York: Ugly Duckling Presse. ISBN 9781937027407.

Mayer, Bernadette (1976). *Poetry*. 130 pages. New York: Kulchur Foundation.

Mayer, Bernadette (1984). *Utopia*. 130+17 pages. New York: United Artists Books.

Mayer, Peter (1979-02-00). *Alphabetical and Letter Poems: A Chrestomathy*. 104 pages. London: The Menard Press. ISBN 9780903400350.

Mayer, Bernadette (2013-03-26). *The Helens of Troy, NY*. 48 pages. New

York: New Directions. ISBN 9780811220422.

McCaffery, Steve (1984). *Panopticon*. 100 pages. Toronto: blewointmentpress. ISBN 9780889710979.

McCaffery, Steve (2001-02-20). *Seven Pages Missing, Volume One: Selected Texts 1969-1999*. 464 pages. Toronto: Coach House Books. ISBN 9781552450499.

McCaffery, Steve (2002-12-20). *Seven Pages Missing, Volume Two: Previously Uncollected Texts 1968-2000*. 384 pages. Toronto: Coach House Books. ISBN 9781552450512.

McCaffery, Steve (2006-06-00). *CRIME SCENES*. 92 pages. London: Veer Books. ISBN 0954688457.

McCaffery, Steve (2007-10-00). *Every Way Oakly (Department of Reissue No. 3.1)*. 104 pages. Toronto: BookThug. ISBN 9781897388266. [First published in 1976.]

McCaffery, Steve (2014-11-00). *Tatterdemalion: A Sketch-Book for Syntax. Derelictions, Poeme Povera, Paralipomena and Semi-demi Texts 1974-2013*. 212 pages. London: Veer Books. ISBN 9781907088728.

McCleary, Ross (2016-02-05). *The Universe is all of Space and its*

Contents. Calgary: Spacecraft Press.

McEwan, Andrew (2012-05-00). *repeater*. 96 pages. Toronto: BookThug. ISBN 9781927040072.

McEwan, Andrew (2016-08-00). *Can't tell if this book is depressing or if I'm just Sad*. Calgary: No press.

McKim, George (2015-08-01). *Found & Lost*. 52 pages. Los Angeles: Silver Birch Press. ISBN 9780692399156.

McLaughlin, Stephen, Carpenter, James, Zykov, Vladimir, Laynor, Gregory, and [Sparks, Kaegan] (2008). *Issue 1*. 3785 pages. Principal Hand Editions; [/ubu editions (Publishing the Unpublishable)].

McLaughlin, Stephen (2014-02-18/19). *Puniverse*. [57 volumes; 158 pages each. Also in TXT and NFO. GPDF Editions.

McQuillin, Anna (2015-02-15). *Wild Woodbine*. [56 pages]. Zürich: LUMA Foundation (1000 BOOKS BY 1000 POETS). ISBN 9781312927612.

Melgard, Holly (2011-03-29). *Poems for Baby Trilogy I: Colors for Baby*. [44 pages]. TROLL THREAD.

Melgard, Holly (2011-03-29). *Poems for Baby Trilogy II: Foods for Baby*. [44 pages]. TROLL THREAD.

Melgard, Holly (2011-03-29). *Poems for Baby Trilogy III: Shapes for Baby*. [44 pages]. TROLL THREAD.

MELGARD, HOLLY (2012-11-15). *THE MAKING OF THE AMERICANS*. 32 pages. TROLL THREAD.

Melgard, Holly (2014). *CATS CAN'T TASTE SUGAR*. [46 pages]. Gauss PDF.

Melnick, David (1983-12-00). *Men in Aida: Book One*. 26 pages. Berkeley: Tuumba Press.

Melnick, David J. (2015-01-00). *Men in Aïda*, with a preface by Sean Gurd. 204 pages. Tirana: Uitgeverij. ISBN 9789491914041.

Melo e Castro, E.M. de (2003). *Antologia para inici-antes: 1950-2002*. 265 pages. Vila Nova da Gaia: Ausência. ISBN 9895530102.

Meltzer, Richard (2000-04-14). *A Whore Just Like The Rest: The Music Writings Of Richard Meltzer*. 608 pages. Cambridge, MA: Da Capo Press. ISBN 9780306809538.

Ménard, Pierre (2009-11-00). *El Ingenioso hidalgo Don Quijote de la Mancha*. 38 pages. Rennes: Éditions Lorem Ipsum. ISBN 9782918829065.

Michel, Fritz, und Abendschein, Hartmut (2015-08-00). *Die Loesung*. Bern: edition taberna kritika. ISBN 9783905846355.

Micleușanu, Mitoș (2012). *Un milion de morți*. București: Tracus Arte. ISBN 9786068361550.

Migone, Christof (2004). *La première phrase et le dernier mot*. 128 pages. Montréal: Le Quartanier. ISBN 2980812250.

Miletic, Philip, and Dodman, Craig (2014-03-16). *world 1-1*. [46 pages]. Zürich: LUMA Foundation (1000 BOOKS BY 1000 POETS). ISBN 9781304953957.

Militaru, Iulia, & Co. (2016). *Confiscarea bestiei. O postcercetare*. 188 pages. București: frACTalia. ISBN 9786069400562.

Millán, Fernando (1993). *La depresión en España*. Madrid: Ediciones Amargord. [Second edition, supplement to no. 5 of *Abreojos* magazine.]

Milutis, Joe (2014-11-00). *Marcel Duchamp's The [Creative] Act*. [14 pages]. Gauss PDF.

Milutis, Joe, feat. Cortes, Amber (2015-07-07). *The Radiotelegrapher's Song*. 48 pages + AIF file. Gauss PDF.

Mirakove, Carol (2004-05-01). *Occupied*. 52 pages. Berkeley: Kelsey Street Press. ISBN 9780932716668.

Moestrup, Mette (2006-09-28). *kingsize*. 69 pages. Oslo: Gyldendal. ISBN 9788702052770.

Mohammad, K. Silem (2003-08-01). *Deer Head Nation*. 120 pages. San Diego: Tougher Disguises Press. ISBN 9780974016702.

Mohammad, K. Silem (2009-07-00). *Sonnagrams 1-20*. 28 pages. Cincinnati: Slack Buddha Press.

Moles, Stephen (2014-10-16). *The Comedy of Hamlet*. [271 pages]. Gauss PDF.

Molina, Feliz (2011). *Nail Hearts Clip: Epistolary Fantasy Blog From 2009-2010*. [33 pages]. /ubu editions (Publishing the Unpublishable).

Molina, Feliz Lucia (2012). *a Letter to Kim Jong-Il Looking at Things*. [147 pages]. Gauss PDF.

Montfort, Nick (2010-10-31). *Riddle & Bind*. Urbana, IL: Spineless Books. ISBN 9780980139273.

Montfort, Nick (2013-02-00). *The First M Numbers*. [4 pages]. Calgary: No press.

Montfort, Nick (2013-12-17). *World Clock*. Harvard Book Store.

Montfort, Nick (2014-06-00). *#!*. 160 pages. Denver: Counterpath Press. ISBN 9781933996462.

Montfort, Nick (2014-11-00). *Megawatt*. Printed on Paige/Harvard Book Store.

Montfort, Nick (2016-10-26). *AUTOPIA*. [256 pages]. TROLL THREAD.

Montfort, Nick, Bouchardon, Serge, Campana, Andrew, Fedorova, Natalia, León, Carlos, Małecka, Aleksandra, and Marecki, Piotr (2016-10-00). *2x6*. 256 pages. Los Angeles: Les Figues Press. ISBN 9781934254677.

Moore, Nicholas (1990). *Spleen*. 60 pages. London: The Menard Press. ISBN 9780951375303. [Second edition?]

Moraga, Clayton (2010-09-16). *Experiment 1*. 780 pages. San Jose: Mauritania Trading Company.

Moriarty, Laura (2010). *A Tonalist*. 150 pages. Callicoon: Nightboat Books. ISBN 9780982264560.

Morris, Simon (2005). *Re-writing Freud*. 752 pages. York: information as material. ISBN 0953676587.

Morris, Simon (2007). *An Intolerable Piece of Writing: Pedagogy As Performed Absence*. 90 pages. /ubu editions (Publishing the Unpublishable).

Morris, Simon (2010). *Getting Inside Jack Kerouac's Head*. 324 pages.

York: information as material. ISBN 9781907468025.

Morris, Simon (2012). *Pigeon Reader*. 300 pages. York: information as material. ISBN 9781907468155.

Morris, Simon, and Thurston, Nick (2008). *Spinning Vol. II: De-Centering the Self*. 24 pages. York: information as material. ISBN 9780955309274.

morrison, yedda (2008-11-30). *girl scout nation*. [Ann Arbor]: displaced press. ISBN 9780982212004.

morrison, yedda (2012-04-24). *Darkness. 132 pages*. Los Angeles: Make Now Press. ISBN 9780981596242.

Morrow, Charlie (2012). *Moving My Vowels*. 26 pages. calmaplombprombombbalm.com.

Moscona, Myriam (2011-09-01). *Negro marfil/Ivory black*, translated by Jen Hofer. 140 pages. Los Angeles: Les Figues Press. ISBN 9781934254226.

Mosconi, Joseph (2008). *33° Houdini*. 17 pages. Los Angeles: PRB Publications.

Mosconi, Joseph (2009). *Galvanized Iron on the Citizens' Band*. 81 pages. Los Angeles: Poetic Research Bureau.

Mosconi, Joseph (2010). *WORD SEARCH*.
OMG! Press.

Mosconi, Joseph (2016-05-03).
Renaissance Realism. [58 pages].
Gauss PDF.

Motte, Warren F. (1998-04-01).
*Oulipo: A Primer of Potential
Literature*. 224 pages. Champaign:
Dalkey Archive Press. ISBN
9781564781871.

Mouré, Eirin (2001-04-01). *Sheep's
Vigil by a Fervent Person: A
Translation of Alberto
Caeiro/Fernando Pessoa's O
Guardador de Rebanhos*. Toronto:
House of Anansi Press. ISBN
9780887846601.

Mouré, Erin (1999). *Pillage Laud*.
108 pages. Toronto: Moveable Type
Books.

Mueller, Kristen (2013-12-00).
*Partially Removing the Remove of
Literature*. Calgary: No press. [A
longer version edited by & So
(2014-02-00); 28 pages.]

Mugavero, Nicolas (2013). *Eight
Million Copies of Moby-Dick*. [1001
pages]. Gauss PDF.

MUGAVERO, NICOLAS (2013-11-20).
*INSTRUCTIONS FOR KILLING YOUR
WIFE*. [140 pages]. TROLL THREAD.

Mugavero, Nicolas (2014). *Restart*.
[137 pages]. Gauss PDF.

Mugavero, Nicolas (2015). *164*. [532 pages]. orworse press.

Mugavero, Nicolas J. (2016-06-28). *LEXICON CETUS*. 670 pages. orworse press. ISBN 9781365223877.

Mullen, Harryette (2002-02-22). *Sleeping with the Dictionary*. 85 pages. Berkeley: University of California Press. ISBN 9780520231436.

Mullen, Harryette (2006). *Recyclopedia: Trimmings, S*PeRM**K*T, and Muse & Drudge*. 176 pages. Saint Paul: Graywolf. ISBN 9781555974565.

Mullen, Laura (2011-03-00). *Dark Archive*. 152 pages. Berkeley: University of California Press. ISBN 9780520268869.

Mullen, Laura (2012-08-15). *Enduring Freedom*. 75 pages. Los Angeles: Otis Books | Seismicity Editions. ISBN 9780984528981.

Murphy, Brian (2014-06-19). *ELSSSUY*. 540 pages. Lulu.com.

Musil, Robert (2016-09-00). *Über die Dummheit (Kolorierte Fassung)*. 48 pages. Bern: edition taberna kritika (kol. F.). ISBN 9783905846416.

Müller, Heidi (2016-02-00). *Unterlassungserklärung*. 8 pages. Bern: edition taberna kritika. ISBN 9783905846379.

Nakayasu, Sawako (2004-10-01). *So We Have Been Given Time Or.* 96 pages. Seattle: Wave Books. ISBN 9780974635309.

Nakayasu, Sawako (2010-03-00). *Texture Notes.* 136 pages. Tucson: Letter Machine Editions. ISBN 9780981522722.

Nardone, Michael (2014-02-05). *TRANSACTION RECORD.* [653 pages]. Gauss PDF.

Neto, Álvaro (1971). *Gramática histórica.* 63 pages. Funchal: Livros CF [Semanário Comércio do Funchal].

Nicolai, Olaf, und Wenzel, Jan (2012). *LABYRINTH: Ein Buch in vier Vorträgen.* 320 pages. Leipzig: Spector Books; Zurich: Rollo Press. ISBN 9783940064820.

Nicolas, Alexa (2014-10-28). *Engineering Body in Seven Parts.* [68 pages]. Zürich: LUMA Foundation (1000 BOOKS BY 1000 POETS). ISBN 9781312634046.

Nielsen, Rasmus Halling (2008-11-20). *Bilag til Niihlsø 98-09.* [2 x 10 pages]. København: Forlaget 28/6. ISBN 9788799268634.

Nilsson, Ulf Karl Olov (2011). *Handlingarna.* 80 pages. Stockholm: Drucksache. ISBN 9789197891332.

[No Credit] (2010). *Book 2 (Version 3).* [12 pages]. Gauss PDF.

Novotný, Pavel (2010). *Mraky*. 48 pages. Praha: Klub přátel Psího vína. ISBN 9788090445437.

Nowak, Mark, and Teh, Ian (2009-04-01). *Coal Mountain Elementary*. 170 pages. Minneapolis: Coffee House Press. ISBN 9781566892285.

Nufer, Doug (2004-08-17). *Never Again*. 202 pages. New York: Black Square Editions; [Thunder's Mouth Press]. ISBN 0971248567. [Previously published digitally in 2002; /ubu editions.]

Nufer, Doug (2006). *Rumor*. 22 pages. /ubu editions (Publishing the Unpublishable).

Nufer, Doug (2013). *Lounge Acts*. 66 pages. Los Angeles: Insert Blanc Press. ISBN 9780981462387.

Nyende, Jasmine (2014). *Tracked and Hacked with HTML*. [9 pages]. Gauss PDF.

[o.w., anna] (2014). *to catch a predator*. xi; 68 pages. orworse press.

O'Sullivan, Maggie (1986-01-00). *From the Handbook of That & Furriery (Piece for Voice & Slides)*. [56 pages]. London: Writers Forum.

Ojeda-Sague, Gabriel (2014-02-18). *JOGS*. 71 pages. Lulu.com.

Olazaval, José Luis Ayala (1984). *Canto Sideral*. 36 pages. Lima: Editorial Juan Meija Baja.

Olmos, Giovanna (2014-10-30). *Gio vanna, gi gio vaNn a*. [76 pages]. Zürich: LUMA Foundation (1000 BOOKS BY 1000 POETS). ISBN 9781312594968.

Olsen, Redell (2012-08-28). *punk faun (a bar rock pastel)*. Berkeley: subpress. ISBN 9781930068568.

"Ondaatje, Michael" (2011-07-11). *Michael Ondaatje on Michael Ondaatje on Lulu*. 29 pages. House of Farts.

Orange, Tom (2008). *American Dialectics*. Cincinnati: Slack Buddha Press.

Orr, Stephanie Pauline (2015-01-10). *Let Me Introduce Myself*. 40 pages. Zürich: LUMA Foundation (1000 BOOKS BY 1000 POETS). ISBN 9781312825567.

Osman, Jena (2010-10-00). *The Network*. 96 pages. New York: Fence Books. ISBN 9781934200407.

Ottinger, Kathleen (2014-11-02). *the mouth sounds such hauntings*. 40 pages. Zürich: LUMA Foundation (1000 BOOKS BY 1000 POETS). ISBN 9781312646810.

Ouředník, Patrik (2001). Europeana: Stručné dějiny dvacátého věku. 126

pages. Praha/Litomyšl: Paseka. ISBN 8071854042.

Paetsch, John (2010). *annotated don cha*. [10 pages]. Gauss PDF.

Paetsch, John (2011). *Crista's Severance Package xxx*. [29 pages]. Gauss PDF. [also (2011). *Crista's Severance Package xxx Supplement*. 1 page. Gauss PDF.]

Paetsch, John (2011). *//only after she mirrored flipt/scripts back into amazing secrets channel did the whole fucking thing become mine//*. [31 pages]. Gauss PDF.

Paetsch, John (2013). *brnt ghst vlnt*. [127 pages]. GPDF Editions.

Paolera, Lucia della (2011). *Instruction Manual*. York: information as material.

PAPARUTZY [Rutzmoser, Jan] (2016-03-20). *Concrete Poetry*. [40 pages]. Lulu.com.

PAPARUTZY [Rutzmoser, Jan] (2016-04-05). *800K VAL#UE*. [800 pages]. Lulu.com.

PAPARUTZY [Rutzmoser, Jan] (2016-04-19). *MILLION DOLLAR MILLION DOLLAR BABY SCRIPT SCRIPT*. [120 pages]. Lulu.com.

PAPARUTZY [Rutzmoser, Jan] (2016-05-14). *LULU*. [86 pages]. Lulu.com.

Parlant, Pierre (2006-05-00). *Précis de nos marqueurs mobiles*. 30

pages. Bordeaux: Éditions de l'Attente. ISBN 9782914688451.

Parrish, Allison (2015-10-13). *@everyword*. The Book. 2338 pages. New York: Instar Books. ISBN 9780990452850.

Pato, Chus (2008-02-08). *Hordas de escritura*. 91 pages. Vigo: Xerais. ISBN 9788497827041.

Patterson, Simon (1994). *Rex Reason*. [110 pages]. London: Book Works. ISBN 9781870699136.

Paul, Cris (2010-04-00). *stenia cultas handbook: maps and annotations*. 76 pages. London: Veer Books. ISBN 9781907088124.

Penberthy, Jenny, ed. (2009-12-00). *The Capilano Review #3-7/ Winter 2009; Less is More: The Poetics of Erasure*. The CapilaNo press Society

Perec, Georges (1969). *La Disparition*. 304 pages. Paris: Éditions Denoël.

Perec, Georges (1982). *Tentative d'épuisement d'un lieu parisien*. Paris: Christian Bourgois. ISBN 2267003260.

Perloff, Marjorie (1994-06-25). *Radical Artifice: Writing Poetry in the Age of Media*. 264 pages. Chicago: University Of Chicago Press. ISBN 9780226657349.

perloff, marjorie (2012-04-15). *unoriginal genius: poetry by other means in the new century*. 232 pages. Chicago: The University of Chicago Press. ISBN 9780226660622.

Perloff, Marjorie, and Dworkin, Craig, eds. (2009). The Poetry of Sound/The Sound of Poetry. 344 pages. Chicago: University of Chicago Press. ISBN 9780226657431.

Pesutic, Sergio (1986). *La hinteligencia militar*. Santiago de Chile.

Peters, Mark (2008). *Men*. 204 pages. /ubu editions (Publishing the Unpublishable).

Petit, Chris (2013-07-00). *GOOGLEmeGOD*. 24 pages. London: Test Centre.

Petrash, Adam (2015-06-11). *a*. Calgary: Spacecraft Press.

Petz, Yuka (2011). *noun*. 27 pages. New Orleans.

Phaneuf, Marc-Antoine K. (2007-08-00). *Fashionably Tales: une épopée des plus brillants exploits*. 200 pages. Montréal: Le Quartanier. ISBN 9782923400303.

Phaneuf, Marc-Antoine K. (2008-08-00). *Téléthons de la Grand Surface (inventaire catégorique)*. 200 pages. Montréal: Le Quartanier. ISBN 9782923400464.

Phaneuf, Marc-Antoine K. (2013-05-00). *Cavalcade en cyclorama*. 74 pages. Montréal: Le Quartanier. ISBN 9782896980871.

Philip, M. NourbeSe (2008). *Zong!*. 224 pages. Middletown: Wesleyan University Press. ISBN 9780819568762.

Phillips, Tom (1970). *A Humument*. [3 pages, 36 leaves of plates]. London: Tetrad Press. (Also see later editions.)

Pichler, Michalis (2008). *Un coup de dés jamais n'abolira le hasard: sculpture*. 32 pages. Berlin: Greatest Hits. ISBN 3978868740011.

Pichler, Michalis (2011). *Some More Sonnet(s)*. 90 pages. Berlin. ISBN 9783868740097. [Also see Carrión, Ulises (1972) and Pichler, Michalis (2014).]

Pichler, Michalis (2014). *555 Schnapspresse Sonnets*. [24 pages]. Leipzig: Lubok Verlag.

Pichler, Michalis (2015-06-01). *The Ego and Its Own*. New York: Ugly Duckling Presse. ISBN 9781937027544.

Pichler, Michalis, Dworkin, Craig, Goldsmith, Kenneth, and Monk, Jonathan (2012). *January 5-31, 2012*. [20 pages]. Berlin.

Pimenta, Alberto (1984). *read&mad*. 40 pages. Lisboa: &etc.

Place, Vanessa (2005-07-31). *Dies: A Sentence*. 145 pages. Los Angeles: Les Figues Press. ISBN 9780976637110.

Place, Vanessa (2008). *La Medusa*. 488 pages. Tuscaloosa: FC2/University of Alabama Press. ISBN 9781573661454.

Place, Vanessa (2008). *Statement of Facts*. [67 pages]. /ubu editions (Publishing the Unpublishable).

Place, Vanessa (2010-04-00). *The Allegory and the Archive*. Calgary: No press.

Place, Vanessa (2010-05-00). *Notes on Why Conceptualism is better than Flarf*. Calgary: No press.

Place, Vanessa (2010-06-00). *Tragodía 1: Statement of Facts*. 430 pages. Los Angeles: Insert Blanc Press. ISBN 9781934254257.

Place, Vanessa (2011-01-00). *Echo*. Calgary: No press.

Place, Vanessa (2011-06-00). *Tragodía 2: Statement of the Case*. 80 pages. Los Angeles: Insert Blanc Press. ISBN 9781934254202.

Place, Vanessa (2011-06-22). *Locus Solus*. 32 pages. ood press. ISBN 9781257799206.

Place, Vanessa (2011-06-23). *Factory Work*. 76 pages. ood press. ISBN 9781257640126.

Place, Vanessa (2011-06-23). *Stoked.* 102 pages. ood press. ISBN 9781257642021.

Place, Vanessa (2011-06-27). *Only Yahweh.* 36 pages. ood press. ISBN 9781257644308.

Place, Vanessa (2011-07-10). *P.O.T.I.C.H.E.* or "*Pathway to Decent Work for Women*". 70 pages. ood press. ISBN 9781257640171.

Place, Vanessa (2011-08-00). *Redaction.* Calgary: No press.

Place, Vanessa (2011-09-00). *Tragodía 3: Argument.* 298 pages. Los Angeles: Insert Blanc Press. ISBN 9781934254202.

Place, Vanessa (2011-09-28). *Le vierge, le vivace et le bel aujourd'hui.* 140 pages. ood press. ISBN 9781257048205.

Place, Vanessa (2011-09-28). *die dichtkunst.* 390 pages. ood press. ISBN 9781257649792.

Place, Vanessa (2011-09-30). *Page Not Found.* 32 pages. ood press. ISBN 9781257640201.

Place, Vanessa (2011-09-30). *The Polished You.* 34 pages. ood press. ISBN 9781257644155.

Place, Vanessa (2011-09-30). *Poems for OodPress.* 34 pages. ood press. ISBN 9781257644292.

Place, Vanessa (2011-10-02). *SCUM Manifesto*. 76 pages. ood press. ISBN 9781257007059.

Place, Vanessa (2011-11-04). *Revolution*. 392 pages. ood press. ISBN 9781257797073.

Place, Vanessa (2012). *[PARROT 11] Forcible Oral Copulation*. 20 pages. Los Angeles: Insert Blanc Press. ISSN 2169381111.

Place, Vanessa (2012-02-22). *Andersens Wank*. Århus: Edition After Hand. ISBN 9788790826154.

Place, Vanessa (2012-06-00). *Like Something in the United States*. Calgary: No press.

Place, Vanessa (2013-02-14). *Boycott*. 120 pages. New York: Ugly Duckling Presse. ISBN 9781937027148.

Place, Vanessa (2013-03-26). *Gone with the Wind*. 309 pages. ood press. ISBN 9781257049042.

Place, Vanessa (2014-04-24). *No More*. Calgary: No press.

Plessis, Michael du (2012-12-03). *The Memoirs of JonBenet by Kathy Acker*. 103 pages. Los Angeles: Les Figues Press. ISBN 9781934254363.

PMatos, Jonay (2015-11-23). *My Father is Mickey Mouse*. [2 pages]. Gauss PDF.

Porter, Bern (1961). *Scandinavian Summer: A Psycho-Visual*

Recollection in Six Languages of a Journey through Norway, Sweden, Finland, Russia, Denmark. [264 pages]. Madison and Huntsville.

Porter, Bern (1966). *468B Thy Future*. [120 pages]. Huntsville.

Porter, Bern (1972). *Waste Maker [1926-1961]*. [316 pages]. Somerville: Abyss Publications.

Porter, Bern (1975). *The Manhattan Telephone Book 1972*. 350 pages. Somerville: Abyss Publications. ISBN 9780911856071.

Porter, Bern (1985). *The Last Acts of Saint Fuck You*. West Lima: Xerox Sutra Editions.

Porter, Bern (1993). *Sounds That Arouse Me: Selected Writings*. 163 pages. Thomaston: Tilbury House. ISBN 9780884481010.

Portugal, Anne (2008). *Quisite Moment*, translated from the French by Rosmarie Waldrop. 24 pages. Providence: Burning Deck Press. ISBN 9781886224957.

Prevallet, Kristin (2002-10-00). *Scratch Sides: Poetry, Documentation, and Image-Text Projects*. 77 pages. Austin: Skanky Possum. ISBN 9780970395238.

Prigov, Dmitri [Дми́трий Алекса́ндрович При́гов] (19--). *Odna tysiacha trista sem'desiat sed'moi grobik otrinutykh stikhov*

[The one thousand three hundred and seventy-seventh little coffin of rejected verse]. Москва [Moscow].

Prince, Richard (2011). *The Catcher in the Rye*. New York: American Place.

pringle, kathyrn l. (2009-01-15). *RIGHT NEW BIOLOGY*. Queens: Factory School. ISBN 9781600010583.

Pritchard, N.H. (1970). *The Matrix. Poems: 1960-1970*. 204 pages. Garden City: Doubleday & Company.

Pritchard, N.H. (1971). *EECCHHOOEESS*. [70 pages]. New York: New York University Press.

Prundaru, Ana (2016-04-00). *Free Dirt is Yours*. [20 pages]. SOd press.

Prundaru, Ana (2016-06-28). *React*. 17 pages. Gauss PDF.

Queneau, Raymond (1947-04-28). *Exercices de style*. 168 pages. Paris: Editions Gallimard.

Queneau, Raymond (1961). *Cent mille milliards de poèmes*. [30 pages]. Paris: Editions Gallimard.

Queneau, Raymond (1975). *Morale élémentaire*. 152 pages. Paris: Gallimard. ISBN 9782070293506.

Quintela, Joseph, ed. (2012-02-09). *SF&D | February 2012 [Black Market]*. 46 pages. Deadly Chaps.

Radon, Lisa (2011). *Sentences on Sentences on Paragraphs on Paragraphs*. 47 pages. Portland: Jank Editions/Publication Studio. ISBN 9781935662747.

Raicovich, Laura (2014-07-00). *A Diary of Mysterious Difficulties*. 100 pages. Portland: Downeaster Editions / Publication Studio. ISBN 9781624620676.

Rankine, Claudia (2014-10-04). *Citizen: An American Lyric*. 166 pages. Minneapolis: Graywolf Press. ISBN 9781555976903.

Ratcliffe, Stephen (1998-04-00). *Mallarmé: Poem in Prose*. 112 pages. Santa Barbara: Santa Barbara Review Publications. ISBN 0965549712.

Ratcliffe, Stephen (2007). *HUMAN / NATURE*. 1003 pages. /ubu editions (Publishing the Unpublishable).

Ratcliffe, Stephen (2011). *Remarks on Color / Sound*. 1000 pages. Editions Eclipse.

Ratcliffe, Stephen (2011). *Temporality*. 1000 pages. Editions Eclipse.

Ratcliffe, Stephen (2013). *c o n t i n u u m*. 1000 pages. Editions Eclipse.

Ratcliffe, Stephen (2016). *sound of wave in channel*. 1000 pages. Editions Eclipse.

rawlings, a[ngela]. (2002-04-19). *Wide Slumber for Lepidopterists*. 88 pages. Toronto: Coach House Books. ISBN 9781552451694.

Read, Rob (2006-01-00). *O SPAM, POAMS: Selected Daily Treated Spam 2003 - 2005*. 100 pages. Toronto: BookThug. ISBN 9780973718171.

Reber, Jacob (2013). *TAPE 181*. [71 pages]. Gauss PDF.

reber, jacob (2016-10-29). *LOBSTER GENESIS*. 120 pages. orworse press. ISBN 9781365495434.

Reber, Jacob (2014-11-09). *No Results*. [73 pages]. Zürich: LUMA Foundation (1000 BOOKS BY 1000 POETS). ISBN 9781312664098.

Reber, Jacob (2016). *[UL7*. [98 pages]. orworse press.

Reber, Jake (2016-12-00). *Drawmatic (No. 2 in 3 Wise Men Series)*. 102 pages. SOd press.

Reddy, Srikanth (2011-02-07). *Voyager*. 144 pages. Berkeley: University of California Press. ISBN 9780520268852.

Redwood-Martinez, Joseph (2011-04-00). *event statements*. 190 pages. Portland: Jank Editions/Publication Studio. ISBN 9781935662495.

Reimer, Karen [writing as Rhymer, Eve] (1996). *Legendary, Lexical, Loquacious Love*. 189 pages.

Chicago: Sara Ranchouse Publishing. ISBN 1888636092.

Reines, Ariana (2006-11-00). *The Cow*. 109 pages. New York: Fence Books. ISBN 9780977106479.

Rejection Group, The [Johnson, Kent?] (2011-04-20). *5 Works*. Habenicht Press.

Retallack, Joan (1998-09-00). *How to Do Things with Words*. 158 pages. Los Angeles: Sun & Moon Press. ISBN 9781557132130.

Retallack, Joan (2010-06-00). *PROCEDURAL ELEGIES / WESTERN CIV CONT'D /*. 120 pages. New York: Roof Books. ISBN 9781931824392.

Renard, Elisa (2014-11-01). *je suis je dispositif*. [24/16 blank pages.] Zürich: LUMA Foundation (1000 BOOKS BY 1000 POETS). ISBN 9781312646674.

Reuterswärd, Carl Fredrik (1961). *På samma gång*. [42/42 blank pages]. [Stockholm]: Bonniers.

Reznikoff, Charles (1965-07-21). *Testimony: The United States 1885-1890 Recitative*. 115 pages. New York: New Directions. [also see definitive edition: (2015-08-26). *Testimony. The United States (1885-1915): Recitative*. 608 pages. Black Sparrow Press. ISBN 9781567925319.]

Rice, Kylan (2015). *CAPTIONS*. 46 pages. Gauss PDF.

Richard, Frances (2012-02-07). *The Phonemes*. 122 pages. Los Angeles: Les Figues Press. ISBN 9781934254325.

Richards, Deborah (2003). *Last One Out*. 93 pages. [Honolulu]: subpress. ISBN 9781930068216.

Riddell, John (2013). [see beaulieu, derek, and Emerson, Lori, eds. (2013).]

Riedo, Dominik (2014-10-00). *Uns trägt das Angesungene*. 88 pages. Bern: edition taberna kritika. ISBN 9783905846317.

Rinne, Cia (2001). *zaroum*. Helsinki. [On-line edition: 2008.]

rinne, cia (2009-07-13). *notes for soloists*. 32 pages. Stockholm: OEI editör. ISBN 9789185905065.

Rinne, Fred (2003). *All My Bands*. San Francisco.

Rivera Garza, Cristina (2013-06-01). *Los muertos indóciles. Necroescrituras y desapropiación*. 279 pages. Ciudad de México: Tusquets Editores. ISBN 9786074214536.

Riviere, Sam (2015-02-05). *Kim Kardashian's Marriage*. 112 pages. London: Faber & Faber. ISBN 9780571321438.

Roberts, Mo-Leeza (2015). *Head*. 160 pages. London: Book Works. ISBN 9781906012670.

Robinson, Sophie (2009-08-01). *a*. 68 pages. Los Angeles: Les Figues Press. ISBN 9781934254103.

Rosenbridge, Bardsley (2016). *To Be, or Not to Be: Paraphrased*. 150 pages. Tirana: Uitgeverij. ISBN 9789491914089.

Rosenfield, Kim (2001-11-08). *Good Morning--Midnight--*. 106 pages. New York: Roof Books. ISBN 9781931824019.

Rosenfield, Kim (2009-02-01). *re: evolution*. 100 pages. Los Angeles: Les Figues Press. ISBN 9781934254080.

Rosenfield, Kim (2012-11-15). *Lividity*. 171 pages. Los Angeles: Les Figues Press. ISBN 9781934254370.

Rosenfield, Kim (2013-04-01). *USO: I'll Be Seeing You*. 128 pages. New York: Ugly Duckling Presse. ISBN 9781937027063.

Rosenkrantz, Linda ([1969]). *Talk*. 223 pages. New York: G. P. Putnams Sons.

Rosenthal, Tracy Jeanne (2015-10-27). *Burning Questions?*. [35 pages]. Gauss PDF.

Roth, Evan (2014). *Since You Were Born*. 212 pages. Brescia: LINK Editions. ISBN 9781291788846.

Roussel, Raymond (1935). *Comment j'ai écrit certains de mes livres*. 446 pages. Paris: Alphonse Lemerre.

Rubinstein, Lev (2014-12-15). *Compleat Catalogue of Comedic Novelties*; translated by Philip Metres and Tatiana Tulchinsky. 448 pages. New York: Ugly Duckling Presse. ISBN 9781937027421.

Ruefle, Mary (2006-04-01). *A Little White Shadow*. 48 pages. Seattle: Wave Books. ISBN 9781933517032.

Russell, Christopher (2013-01-14). *Pattern Book*. 104 pages. Los Angeles: Insert Blanc Press. ISBN 9780981462370.

Russo, Emmalea (2014). *they*. [58 pages]. Gauss PDF.

Rutkoski, Mark (2013-02-15). *Words of Love*. Los Angeles: Les Figues Press. ISBN 9781934254394.

Rutzmoser, Jon (2014). *TanLin.es/tan_lin*. [146 pages]. Gauss PDF.

Rutzmoser, Jon (2014-09-16). *The Voice Inside The Voice Inside My Head By James Franco*. 37 pages. Lulu.com. ISBN 9781312527225.

Rutzmoser, Jon (2016-03-20). [see PAPARUTZY.]

San Francisco Guerrilla Opera Company, The (2011-03-19). *A Night At The Opera With Hosni Mubarak Hosted By Dave Eggers*. 85 pages. HELPINGER Press.

Sanders, James, & Selvidge, John (2012-10-12). *Walmart Entanglement 3*. 36 poets. Gauss PDF.

Sandri, Giovanna (2014-01-16). *only fragments found: selected poems, 1969-1998; translated from the Italian by Guy Bennett, Faust Pauluzzi, and Giovanna Sandri*. 336 pages. Los Angeles: Otis Books | Seismicity Editions. ISBN 9780986017315.

Sanouillet, Michel, and Peterson, Elmer, eds. (1975). *Salt Seller/Marchand du Sel: The Essential Writings of Marcel Duchamp*. 196 pages. London: Thames and Hudson. ISBN 0500270538.

Sarduy, Severo (1973). *Big Bang: para situar en órbita cinco máquinas de Ramón Alejandro/pour situer en orbite cinq machines de Ramón Alejandro*. 72 pages. Montpellier: Fata Morgana.

[Saroyan, Aram] (1967). *GERTRUDE STEIN*. [24/24 blank pages]. [Cambridge, MA]: LINES.

Saroyan, Aram (1969). *Pages*. [46/48 blank pages]. New York: Random House.

Saroyan, Aram (1970). *THE BEATLES*. [12 pages]. Boston: Barn Dream Press.

Saroyan, Aram (1971). *I AM ROSE*. [15 pages]. Los Angeles: Mini-Books, Inc.

Saroyan, Aram (1971). *MY MUMMY'S DEAD*. [15 pages]. Los Angeles: Mini-Books, Inc.

Saroyan, Aram (2007-05-01). *Complete Minimal Poems*. 280 pages. New York: Ugly Duckling Presse. ISBN 9781933254258.

Saure, Heikki (2011-08-31). *Kirjoituksia maasta*. 324 pages. Helsinki: ntamo. ISBN 9789522151148.

Savarus, Albert (2013). *L'Ambitieux par amour*. 42 pages. Rennes: Éditions Lorem Ipsum. ISBN 9782918829072.

Scheps, Manya (2012). *Available Gmail.com Email Addresses of United States Federal Agencies*. [11 pages]. Gauss PDF.

Schérer, Jacques (1957). *Le «Livre» de Mallarmé*. 440 pages. Paris: Editions Gallimard.

Scherübel, Klaus (2008). *Jack Torrance's All Work and No Play*. [ca. 600 pages].

Schimmel, Seth (2014-03-18). *ASSIGNMENTS*. Zürich: LUMA

Foundation (1000 BOOKS BY 1000 POETS). ISBN 9781304954374.

Schluter, Kit (2013). *without is a part of origin*. [318 pages]. Gauss PDF.

Schlüter, Kit (2014-09-22). *Translations of Forgetting*. [379 pages]. Zürich: LUMA Foundation (1000 BOOKS BY 1000 POETS). ISBN 9781312598133.

Schmaltz, Eric (2014). *EVERYDAY IS BLACK FRIDAY*. 18 pages. Gauss PDF.

Schmaltz, Eric (2014-06-27). *Pages Loading*. Calgary: No press.

Schmidt, Arno, and Riedo, Dominik (2010-11-00). *Obig mét Goldrand*. 56 pages. Bern: edition taberna kritika. ISBN 9783905846119.

Schmitt, Joachim Georg (2009). *Ingredients*. 21 pages. /ubu editions (Publishing the Unpublishable).

Schneiderman, Davis (2013-10-00). *[SIC]: a novel*. 154 pages. Los Angeles: Jaded Ibis Press. ISBN 9781937543372.

Schultz, Susan M. (2008-04-01). *Dementia Blog*. 135 pages. San Diego: Singing Horse Press. ISBN 9780935162417.

Sekiguchi, Ryoko (2008-06-00). *études vapeur suivi de série Grenade*. 48 pages. Coutras: Le Bleu du ciel. ISBN 9782915232523.

Serup, Martin Glaz (2010-11-24). *Marken: Et digt*. 104 pages. Århus: Edition After Hand. ISBN 9788787489799.

Shaw, Lytle (1998). *Principles of the Emeryville Shellmound*. 21 pages. New York: Shark Books. ISBN 0966487125.

Sheppard, Robert (2016-01-00). *Unfinish*. 56 pages. London: Veer Books. ISBN 9781907088803.

Shields, David (2010-02-23). *Reality Hunger: A Manifesto*. 240 pages. New York: Knopf. ISBN 0307273539.

Shirinyan, Ara (2007). *Speech Genres 1-2*. 108 pages. /ubu editions (Publishing the Unpublishable).

Shirinyan, Ara (2008). *Direct Plot*. 36 pages. Oslo: Forlaget Attåt.

Shirinyan, Ara (2008-03-00). *Handsome Fish Offices*. 68 pages. Los Angeles: Insert Blanc Press. ISBN 0981462308.

Shirinyan, Ara (2008-10-15). *Your Country Is Great: Afghanistan-Guyana*. 129 pages. New York: Futurepoem Books. ISBN 9780971680081.

Shirinyan, Ara (2014-01-29). *Julia's Wilderness*. [106 double pages]. Los Angeles: Poetic Research Bureau.

Shirinyan, Ara (2014-10-00). *[PARROT 22] Erotic in Czech Republic*. 16

pages. Los Angeles: Insert Blanc Press. ISSN 2169381122.

Silliman, Ron (2007-04-00). *The Age of Huts (compleat)*. 324 pages. Berkeley: University of California Press. ISBN 9780520250161.

Silliman, Ron (2014-05-00). *Against Conceptual Poetry*. 200 pages. Denver: Counterpath Press. ISBN 9781933996455.

Simpson, Natalie (2010-10-14). *Smash Swizzle Fizz*. [8 pages]. Calgary: No press.

Sink, Jim (2011). *Stanzas for the White Queen*. [26 pages]. Gauss PDF.

Siyun, Zhao (赵思运) (2003). *毛泽东语录（12 首）－ 非虚构实验文本（附评论）》[Quotations of Mao Zedong (12 poems) — Non-Fabricated Experimental Texts (with critiques)]*.

Smart, Willy (2013). *How to Listen to and Understand Fake Music*. 180 pages. Portland: Jank Editions/Publication Studio. ISBN 9781624620478.

Smart, Willy, & Wilner, Brandon (2015-02-21). *Acknowledgements*. 142 pages. Portland: Jank Editions / Publication Studio. ISBN 9781624621017.

Smith, Frank (2010-04-01). *Guantanamo*. 128 pages. Paris: Seuil. ISBN 9782021020953.

Smith, Casey (2010). *Opulent Stone Moccasins*. 269 pages. /ubu editions (Publishing the Unpublishable).

Smith, Janey (2011-10-00). *Janey Smith Stares into Space*. [18 pages]. calmaplombprombombbalm.com.

Smith, Michael V., and Ellingsen, David (2010-08-00). *Body of Text*. 168 pages. Toronto: BookThug. ISBN 9781897388280.

Smith, Rachel (2013-02-22). *White Noise*. 32 pages. Lulu.com.

Snelson, Danny (2015-02-08). *Epic Lyric Poem, 167121 Songs, 257.8 MB File*. [48 pages + SQL, TXT]. TROLL THREAD.

Snelson, Danny (2015-05-28). *EXE TXT*. 244 pages + TXT and ZIP. GPDF Editions. ISBN 9780816650439 [?]

Snelson, Danny (2016-09-15). *Radios*. Make Now Books.

Société Réaliste (2014-09-26). *The Best American Book of the 20th Century*. 128 pages. Eindhoven: Onomatopee. ISBN 9789491677267.

Sommer, Carol (2016-07-01). *An A – Z of Orientations identified within the Novels of Iris Murdoch*. 464

pages. York: information as material. ISBN 9781907468254.

Søndergaard, Morten (2010). *Ordapotek*. [Translated in English by Barbara Haveland; (2012-11-00). *Wordpharmacy*. Toronto: BookThug. ISBN 9783943196054.]

Spahr, Juliana (1996). *Response*. 97 pages. Los Angeles: Sun & Moon Press. ISBN 9781557132895.

Spoerri, Daniel (1970). *The Mythological Travels of a Modern Sir John Mandeville, being an account of the Magic, Meatballs and other Monkey Business Peculiar to the Sojourn of Daniel Spoerri on the Isle of Symi, together with divers speculations thereon*, translated out of the French and introduced by Emmett Williams. 278 pages. New York: Something Else Press. ISBN 087110041X.

Spoerri, Daniel (1995-04-00). *Anecdoted Topography of Chance [1962/66]: Probably Definitive Re-Anecdoted Version (Atlas Arkhive, No. 4: Documents of the Avant-Garde)*. London: Atlas Press. ISBN 9780947757885.

Ståhl, Ola (2013-01-28). *Exercizes (Louis-Ferdinand Céline)*. Calgary: No press.

Steck, Ed (2013-11-15). *The Garden: Synthetic Environment for Analysis and Simulation.* 104 pages. New York: Ugly Duckling Presse. ISBN 9781937027230.

Stefans, Brian Kim (2006). *What Is Said to the Poet Concerning Flowers.* 144 pages. Queens: Factory School. ISBN 9781600010484.

Stefans, Brian Kim (2007). *Booty, Egg On: Uncollected Poems and Collaborations.* 327 pages. Philadelphia: Arras Media. ISBN 9780615154510.

Stefans, Brian Kim (2007). *Kluge: A Meditation and other works.* 126 pages. New York: Roof Books. ISBN 9781931824248.

Stefans, Brian Kim (2014-01-00). *Conceptual Writing: The L.A. Brand.* 14 pages. Los Angeles: Area Sneaks.

Sterling, Andy (2013-02-24). *Supergroup.* [426 pages]. GPDF Editions.

Stewart, Michael (2009-10-01). *Almost Perfect Forms.* 26 pages. New York: Ugly Duckling Presse.

Stork, Betty (2011). *Selected Rhyme Schemes of A. E. Housman, Second Version.* [15 pages]. Gauss PDF.

"Strivinski, Igir" (2014-03-29). *IITIBIIGRIPHI IF IGIR STRIVINSKI.* [142 pigis]. Zirich: LIMI Fiinditiin (1000 BIIKS BI 1000

PIITS). ISBN 9781304992178. [also see Comitta, Tom (2015-04-27)].

Suárez, Angelo V. (2013-10-31). *Interview*. 174 pages. Lulu.com.

Suárez, Angelo V. (2013-11-01). *Circuit: The Blurb Project [2012]*. 76 pages. Lulu.com.

Suárez, Angelo V. (2013-11-01). *Composition by Boggle: 52 Confessions*. 60 pages. Lulu.com.

Suárez, Angelo V. (2013-11-01). *Maliit lang 'yung sa 'yo, itabi mo, magpadaan ka: Adventures in parataxis*. 36 pages. Lulu.com.

Suárez, Angelo V. (2013-11-25). *Ariane: a stock epic*. 133 pages. Lulu.com.

Suárez, Angelo V. (2014-09-26). *Poem of Diminishing Poeticity*. 40 pages. GPDF Editions.

Suárez, Angelo V. (2015-02-23). *Philippine English: A Novel*. 314 pages. GPDF Editions.

Sullivan, Gary (2001-11-00). *How to Proceed in the Arts*. 102 pages. Cambridge, MA: Faux Press. ISBN 9780971037113.

Sullivan, Gary (2008-04-01). *PPL IN A DEPOT*. 100 pages. New York: Roof Books. ISBN 9781931824286.

Sundin, Kajsa (2007). *Definition*. Stockholm: OEI editör. ISBN 9197601467

Surani, Moez (2016-10-17). ةيلمع *Operación Opération Operation* 作 戰 Операция. 112 pages. Toronto: BookThug. ISBN 9781771662680.

Swensen, Cole (2008-04-08). *Ours.* 118 pages. Berkeley: University of California Press. ISBN 9780520941564.

Swereda, Robert (2014-12-17). *CAPTURE.* Calgary: Spacecraft Press.

SYLVESTER, CHRIS (2010). *GRID.* [130 pages]. TROLL THREAD.

SYLVESTER, CHRIS (2010). *THE REPUBLIC.* [466 pages]. TROLL THREAD.

SYLVESTER, CHRIS (2010). *BIOGRAPHY: THERE PAST.* [130 pages]. TROLL THREAD.

SYLVESTER, CHRIS (2011-11-09). *TOTAL WALKTHROUGH.* [664 pages]. TROLL THREAD.

Sylvester, Chris (2012). *CAT MOM ABCDEFGHIJKLMNOPQRSTUVWXYZ.* [691 pages]. Gauss PDF.

SYLVESTER, CHRIS (2012-03-19). *JUNK ROOMS.* 76 pages. TROLL THREAD.

SYLVESTER, CHRIS (2013-02-04). *STILL LIFE WITH THE POKÉMON YELLOW VERSION TEXT DUMP IN 30 PT. MONACO FONT JUSTIFIED TO MARGIN DISTRIBUTED AS A PDF OR A BOOK CONVERTED FROM A MICROSOFT WORD*

DOCUMENT BY CHRIS SYLVESTER 2012/2013. [691 pages]. TROLL THREAD.

SYLVESTER, CHRIS (2013-02-11). *MCNUGGET*. [528 pages]. TROLL THREAD.

SYLVESTER, CHRIS (2013-10-21). *STILL LIFE W/ BLOG 07/12/13 04:24PM // 05:12PM // 264 pgs MSWORD // 10/18/13 // 3:45PM // 595 pgs MSWORD*. [595 pages]. TROLL THREAD.

SYLVESTER, CHRIS (2013-11-22). *ALL DOGS GO TO HELL*. [504 pages]. TROLL THREAD.

SYLVESTER, CHRIS (2013-12-18). *THE_WORLD // OR: THE REPUBLIC II*. [464 pages]. TROLL THREAD.

SYLVESTER, CHRIS (2014). *BOOKS_ABT_THINGS.zip*. Gauss PDF.

Sylvester, Chris (2015-03-16). *caps 0w - 146w, iPhone 6+, 0w 2015, Provider/Processor 'Chris Sylvester'*. GPDF Editions.

SYLVESTER, CHRIS (2015-05-14). *BRAIN BRAIN ORGAN_PLATFORM TORTURE*. [624 pages]. TROLL THREAD.

SYLVESTER, CHRIS (2015-11-18). *BABY-CHRIS: EVOLUTION*. [300 pages]. TROLL THREAD.

SYLVESTER, CHRIS, and YEAROUS-ALGOZIN, JOEY (2012-08-15). *POETRY WALL STREET*. TROLL THREAD.

Szczepaniak, Angela (2011-04-00). *The QWERTY Institute (Annual*

Report). 234 pages. Toronto: BookThug. ISBN 9781897388822.

Šanda, Michal (1998). *Hovězí srdce*. 36 pages. České Budějovice: Velarium. ISBN 8023839276.

Šanda, Michal (1998). *Metro*. 51 pages. Praha: Protis. ISBN 8085940485.

Šanda, Michal, Šofar, Jakub, and Štengl, Petr (2013). *3,14čo!*. Praha: Petr Štengl. ISBN 9788087563120.

Tabios, Eileen R. (2016-10-01). *Amnesia: Somebody's Memoir*. 80 pages. Black Radish Books. ISBN 9780996400169.

Tardos, Anne (2015-08-28). *Nine*. 148 pages. Buffalo: BlazeVOX [books]. ISBN 9781609642266.

Tardy, Nicolas (2010-10-10). *Les ready-mades textuels*. 72 pages. Genève: HEAD (Haute Ecole d'Art et de Design de Genève). ISBN 9782970062349.

Tardy, Nicolas (2011-06-00). *un homme tout juste vivant - pays des merveilles*. 52 pages. Bordeaux: Éditions de l'Attente. ISBN 9782362420122.

Tegeder, Dannielle (2008). *Falling Apart NYC*. [62 pages]. /ubu editions (Publishing the Unpublishable).

Terhaar, Tim (2014-11-18). *Not Marx*. 38 pages. Gauss PDF.

Théval, Gaëlle (2015-10-00). *Poésies ready-made, XXe-XXIe siècles*. 288 pages. Paris: L'Harmattan.

Thörn, Pär (2007-02-00). *Inventeringen*. 52 pages. Stockholm: OEI editör. ISBN 9789197601450.

Thörn, Pär (2010). *Röda Rummet (alfabetisk)*. 228 pages. Stockholm: Drucksache. ISBN 9789197891356.

Thörn, Pär (2012). *Verkligheten nedtecknas, ges ord, förvanskas och blir del av en ny omformad verklighet: dokument kring mordet på Robert Risberg i Uddevalla 960513*. Orosdi Back. ISBN 9789186593346.

Thörn, Pär (2012-03-10). *Die Leiden des jungen Werthers (alphabetisch)*. 90 pages. [Malmö]: Storno Förlag. ISBN 919800090X.

Thörn, Pär (2016-08-04). *Vattna vargen*. 130 pages. Diskret Förlag. ISBN 9789163910401.

Thurston, Nick (2006). *Reading the Remove of Literature*. 228 pages. York: information as material. ISBN 9780955309212.

Thurston, Nick (2007). *Historia Abscondita (An Index of Joy)*. 24

pages. York: information as material. ISBN 9780955309267.

Thurston, Nick (2013). *Of the Subcontract: or Principles of Poetic Right*. Foreword: McKenzie Wark / Afterword: Darren Wershler. 144 pages. York: information as material. ISBN 9781907468186.

Tiberg, Joar [--j-o-a-a-r-t-i-b-e-r-g-] (2008). *---t--m-p-t--*. 16 pages. Oslo: Forlaget Attåt.

Tiberg, Joar (2010-08-00). *Ansvaret Ansvaret Ansvaret Ansvaret*. 743 pages. Stockholm: Albert Bonniers Förlag. ISBN 9789100122492.

TIERNEY, ORCHID (2016-04-16). *earsay*. [25 pages]. TROLL THREAD.

Timmons, Mathew (2006-12-00). *She*. 152 pages. Los Angeles: Insert Blanc Press.

Timmons, Mathew (2009-09-00). *CREDIT*. 800 pages. Los Angeles: Insert Blanc Press; Lulu. ISBN 9780981462349.

Timmons, Mathew (2010-12-01). *The New Poetics*. 112 pages. Los Angeles: Les Figues Press. ISBN 9781934254158.

Timmons, Mathew (2014-11-00). *[PARROT 23] Complex Textual Legitimacy Proclamation*. Los Angeles: Insert Blanc Press. ISSN 2169381123.

Tiravanija, Rirkit (2015). *DO NOT EVER WORK*. 102 pages. Paris: onestar press.

Tixador, Laurent (2013-09-00). *Quelques bons moments de bricolage*. 96 pages. Paris: Manuella éditions. ISBN 9782917217511.

Toder, Emily (2016-09-27). *Aging*. 170 pages. GPDF Editions.

"Torrance, Jack" (2008-12-18). *All Work And No Play Makes Jack A Dull Boy: The Masterpiece Of A Well-Known Writer With No Readers...* 128 pages. Gengotti Editore. ISBN 9788887381078.

"Torrance, Jack" [Buehler, Phil] (2008-12-22). *All Work and No Play Makes Jack a Dull Boy (Wendy Torrance Cover)*. 80 pages. Blurb.

Torre, Mónica de la (2008-11-00). *Public Domain*. 97 pages. New York: Roof Books. ISBN 9781931824309.

Toscano, Rodrigo (2004). *To Leveling Swerve*. 77 pages. San Francisco: Krupskaya Books. ISBN 9781928650232.

Trecartin, Ryan (2009). *K-CoreaINC.K (Section A)*. 41 pages. /ubu editions (Publishing the Unpublishable).

Trevino, Hermes (2014-02-25). *Hermes Germé*. [40 pages]. Zürich: LUMA

Foundation (1000 BOOKS BY 1000 POETS). ISBN 9781312048744.

Troyan, Cassandra (2016). *A Theory in Tears (ANNOTATIONS & CASES FOR FREEDOM & PROSTITUTION)*. Chicago: Kenning Editions.

Turnbull, Alison (2002). *Spring Snow - A Translation*. 152 pages. London: Book Works. ISBN 9781870699594.

Turner, Michael (2011-04-00). *Free Concert*. 54 pages. Vancouver: Bookmachine/Publication Studio. ISBN 9780986709920.

Tuten, Frederic (1971). *The Adventures of Mao on the Long March*. 121 pages. Citadel Press. ISBN 0806502487.

Tysdal, Daniel Scott (2015-09-15). *Fauxccasional Poems*. 98 pages. Fredericton: Goose Lane Editions / icehouse poetry. ISBN 9780864928726.

Uribe, Sara (2012). *Antígona González*. [116 pages]. Oaxaca de Juárez: Sur+ ediciones.

Urquidi, AJ (2014-02-20). *The Patterned Fragment*. 84 pages. Zürich: LUMA Foundation (1000 BOOKS BY 1000 POETS). ISBN 9781312034136.

Ugilt, Christoffer (2014-12-10). *Individ i fællesskab 1*. 240 pages.

Århus: Antipyrine. ISBN 9788793108219.

Valencia, Jacqueline (2014-04-00). *text one*. 11 pages. Lulu.com [?].

Valencia, Jacqueline (2014-06-07). *ULYSSES*. Calgary: No press.

Valéry, Françoise (2002-09-00). *Victimes du Genre, un livre co-produit avec l'école des Beaux-Arts de Bordeaux*. 158 pages. Bordeaux: Éditions de l'Attente. ISBN 9782914688024.

Valinsky, Michael (2014-02-13). *.TXT*. [62 pages]. Zürich: LUMA Foundation (1000 BOOKS BY 1000 POETS). ISBN 9781312012448.

Valinsky, Rachel (2014-02-15). *art&education*. [60 pages]. Zürich: LUMA Foundation (1000 BOOKS BY 1000 POETS). ISBN 9781312017320.

valoch, jiri (1969-01-00). *8 SONNETS /i have forgotten the song/*. [10 pages]. Toronto: GANGLIA PRESS.

Van Buskirk, Todd (2008-10-08). *The Celestial Marketplace of Lutefisk: A Novel*. 338 pages. Tucson: Liver Pizza Press. ISBN 9781466415744.

Van Buskirk, Todd (2011-08-25). *Born This Date and Died That Date: A Classical Music Forum Talks 18th Century*. 134 pages. Liver Pizza Press. ISBN 9781466252448.

Van Buskirk, Todd (2011-08-25). *Richard Catholic Susan Protestant:*

A Novel. 276 pages. Liver Pizza Press. ISBN 9781466262850.

Van Buskirk, Todd (2011-09-11). *John Marshall High School 1989: A Novel.* 252 pages. Liver Pizza Press. ISBN 9781466321434.

Van Buskirk, Todd (2011-09-16). *There is a comic panel on p.90.* 298 pages. Liver Pizza Press. ISBN 9781466249875.

Van Buskirk, Todd (2011-09-17). *Soul Made Beautiful: A Novel.* 258 pages. Liver Pizza Press. ISBN 9781466335356.

Van Buskirk, Todd (2011-09-23). *There are two comic book panels on p.76.* 134 pages. Tucson: Liver Pizza Press. ISBN 9781466361508.

Van Buskirk, Todd (2011-10-01). *There is a sentence on p.120.* 298 pages. Liver Pizza Press. ISBN 9781466388833.

Van Buskirk, Todd (2011-10-02). *A paragraph on every page except p.120.* 384 pages. Liver Pizza Press. ISBN 9781466393295.

Van Buskirk, Todd (2011-10-22). *Living in Utah With My Husband and Two Kids.* 226 pages. Liver Pizza Press. ISBN 9781466461390.

Van Buskirk, Todd (2011-10-22). *Arctic White Lifetime: The Life and Times of Composer Clarence*

Wahlberg. 272 pages. Liver Pizza Press. ISBN 9781466470378.

Van Buskirk, Todd (2012-01-31). *Old Wig*. 210 pages. Liver Pizza Press. ISBN 9781469964409.

Van Buskirk, Todd (2012-02-29). *Four dollars and thirty-three cents: A Novel*. 254 pages. Liver Pizza Press. ISBN 9781470159559.

Van Buskirk, Todd (2012-03-07). *Untitled Skin*. 158 pages. Liver Pizza Press. ISBN 9781470193041.

Van Buskirk, Todd (2012-03-10). *False Barnyard*. 172 pages. Liver Pizza Press. ISBN 9781466304697.

Van Buskirk, Todd (2012-05-29). *down to a T*. 344 pages. Liver Pizza Press. ISBN 9781477551646.

Van Buskirk, Todd (2012-05-29). *Emily With A Vengeance*. 260 pages. Liver Pizza Press. ISBN 9781105826610.

Van Buskirk, Todd (2012-06-16). *Libertarianism in the Works of Madonna*. 174 pages. Liver Pizza Press. ISBN 9781477669228.

Van Buskirk, Todd (2012-09-06). *swimminghorses*. 194 pages. Liver Pizza Press. ISBN 9781479254576.

Van Buskirk, Todd (2012-10-02). *Unperfect Actor*. 654 pages. Liver Pizza Press. ISBN 9781479270217.

Van Buskirk, Todd (2012-10-15). *Purple Chick*. 818 pages. Liver Pizza Press. ISBN 9781480107618.

Van Buskirk, Todd (2012-11-15). *the above named person*. 206 pages. Liver Pizza Press. ISBN 9781300373360.

Van Buskirk, Todd (2013-06-04). *Research Paper: a novel*. 206 pages. Liver Pizza Press. ISBN 9781300411086.

Van Buskirk, Todd (2015-10-06). *The sentence printed at the top of p.14 is Duplicated in the middle of p.168 and bottom of p.544 within the Context of a 234,348 word text (see p.6 through 609 excluding the Three pages mentioned above.) On p.544 the sentence Bleeds onto p.545. [a novel]*. 612 pages. Liver Pizza Press. ISBN 9781329436855.

Van Buskirk, Todd (2015-11-30). *A birth date, first name, activity and place are determined for each character. Each clue is printed on one page (pages 203 through 215). The birth dates are listed on p.57, the first names on p.463, the activities on p.567, and the places on p.654. [a novel]*. 712 pages. Liver Pizza Press. ISBN 9781312917217.

Van Buskirk, Todd (2016-05-12). *The Sound of the Given Name 'Angela' is three syllables (the first syllable is accented). The name Itself is located Individually on page 428. The header and the page number (printed on each page starting on p.7) are intentionally left off of p.428 [poems].* 648 pages. Liver Pizza Press. ISBN 9781312893702.

Van Buskirk, Todd (2016-05-12). *They place his given-name ("Todd") on pages 25 through 58. Then they place his middle names ("Earl") on p.322 and ("Winkels") on pages 356 through 411. Then they place his Catholic confirmation name ("Augustine") on p.455. After that they place his surname ("Van Buskirk") on pages 500 and 637. [autobiography].* 642 pages. Liver Pizza Press.

Van Buskirk, Todd (2016-05-14). *One 258,226 word sentence begins on p.11, continues on p.205, and ends on p.592 [three novels].* 592 pages. Liver Pizza Press. ISBN 9781365113321.

Van Buskirk, Todd (2016-06-01). *The paragraph that is printed on page 9 and reprinted on pages 10 thru 356 is not seen on pages 1 thru 8, and page 123 [a novel].* 356 pages.

Mankato: Liver Pizza Press. ISBN 9781329093799.

Van Buskirk, Todd (2016-06-04). *Examples of 2 sentence paragraphs are located on pages 33, 53, 56, 79 and 80, and collected into a monologue on p.340 [a play].* 354 pages. Mankato: Liver Pizza Press.

Van Buskirk, Todd (2016-06-19). *Fig.7 shows a comparison of settings by Zollner and Schubert in Wilhelm Muller's "Das Wandern," the first measure of Fig.7 is printed on p.139, the last measure of Fig.7 is printed on p.202 (each measure of Fig.7 is separated by two blank pages) [song cycle].* 358 pages. Mankato: Liver Pizza Press. ISBN 9781329093799.

Van Buskirk, Todd (2016-06-19). *Figure 8 (see page 377) is a piano score (or Orchestral Reduction) of Measures 1 through 14 from Anton Webern's Symphony Op.21 (see Figure 7 on pages 144 and 654). [piano concerto].* 686 pages. Mankato: Liver Pizza Press.

Van Buskirk, Todd (2016-06-28). *A 'Period' (two four-bar phrases) in Beethoven's Piano Sonata in C Minor, Op.13 (Pathetique) second movement is illustrated in fig.8, which is printed on each page for thirty pages, starting on p.11 [piano sonata].* 300 pages. Mankato: Liver Pizza Press. ISBN 9781329007598.

Van Buskirk, Todd (2016-06-28). *Forty-eight original (hand drawn) one panel scenes are reused (or modified to add new dialogue and narration) to create (at two panels per page) a 305 page narrative. How many panels are nestled between pages 44 through 350? [a graphic novel].* 432 pages. Mankato: Liver Pizza Press. ISBN 9781329146198.

Van Buskirk, Todd (2016-07-12). *The word "Pink" is printed at the bottom left of p.32, followed (on p.33) by a 49,288 word excerpt from "The Pink Bunny"; on p.473 "Bunny" is printed at the bottom of the page (at left) followed by a sentence on p.474 [a novel].* 496 pages. Mankato: Liver Pizza Press. ISBN 9781312898561.

Van Buskirk, Todd (2016-07-23). *Carl Schuricht conducts the beginning at around quarter=100 but veers as high as quarter=120 (see fig.1 on p.233). Then, at around bar 54 he bursts ahead to nearly a quarter=140 (see fig.2 on p.335). As he approaches the 2nd theme, at bar 95 he pulls back in a beautifully managed maneuver, to* around a quarter=95 (see fig.3 on p.350). The circled examples (see fig.4) on p.11 reveal Schuricht's care in voicing, highlighting the continuity of the violin line to the celli/bass in bars 129-30, and then a wildly personal dynamic modification in the form of an unwritten crescendo by the brass in bar 135 (see circled example in fig.5 on p.145). [symphony]. 366 pages. Mankato: Liver Pizza Press.

Van Buskirk, Todd (2016-08-07). a Fake Vincent Van Gogh (1853-90) landscape is located on p.168 and 169 as a double-page spread. The Margin of the gutter divides the Image in two. The dimensions of the image on p.168 are 1042 X 1024 pixels and the image on p.169 is 1005 X 1024 pixels. The two images are printed in Black and White. [biography of Vincent van Gogh]. 364 pages. Mankato: Liver Pizza Press. ISBN 9781312995444.

Van Buskirk, Todd (2016-09-29). 31 measures of Wolfgang Mozart's String Quartet No.16 in E-flat major, K.428/421b are on page 125 [string quartet]. 366 pages. Mankato: Liver Pizza Press. ISBN 9781365318849.

Van Buskirk, Todd (2016-12-07). Librarians collaborated with

teachers to refine questions and develop data collection methods that are shown in table 1 (see p.17). Every six school days, 36 students attended an "Advisory" class in which they were taught one of ten pivotal lessons outlined in figure 3 (p.13). After the Final Drafts were submitted (see Appendix starting on p.225), 36 students completed questionnaires (see figure 4 on p.503). Table 2 (p.127) summarizes the data. The remaining (numbered) pages are intentionally left blank (except for the header at the top). [memoirs]. 580 pages. Mankato: Liver Pizza Press. ISBN 9781365559709.

Van Buskirk, Todd (2017-01-01). *A small (0.9) Earth-mass, very temperate (67 °F.) high-manganese rocky silicate planet with almost 1.3 times the expected density and gravity and a coreless silicate moon. It has a hydrosphere of chilled iron pentacarbonyl slush actively cycling with a 0.6 atmosphere of reactive gasses with low-lying dull ebon fog and extreme winds with seasonal driving rain. It is primarily dominated by a titanic placid deep symmetrical ocean (see page 57)* and a titanic symmetrical supercontinent dominated by enmeshed ruddy furrows (p.89) and isolated regions spotted with hundreds of compressed dull black volcanos (page 117). The surface material is otherwise beige mud spotted with light blue-green boulders. // A small Kingdom is built on salt boulders and purple manganese ore. The waters around the kingdom swirl with the Curse of the Iron Slush. The Queen along with her people, elves, and dragons worship the moon which was mysteriously hollowed at its core centuries ago. Legend says the Iron Slush corrupted the core of the moon before the time of The Madness. Now the Kingdom suffers an atmosphere of low-lying fog and extreme winds with seasonal driving rain. The Queen must wander until she discovers the continent (known as The Land Around The Kingdom) marked by the Brown Mud spotted with light blue-green boulders. When she arrives in The Land Around The Kingdom (dominated by a titanic ocean [see page 357] and a titanic supercontinent dominated by enmeshed ruddy furrows [p.489] and isolated regions spotted with *hundreds of compressed dull black volcanos [page 517]) she must find and "Realize the Black Volcano that holds the Enlightenment of The Full Moon." [two novels in one volume].* 584 pages. Mankato: Liver Pizza Press. ISBN 9781365644542.

Van Buskirk, Todd, ed. (2017-01-01). *Four men enter the restroom and see 7 urinals. The first two men choose urinals 1 and 7 (represented by p.7-45 and p.241-280). The Third Man chooses urinal 4 (or p.124-133). The Fourth Man uncomfortably chooses urinal 5 (p.58-122). Pages (with a number printed on the bottom of the page) not Mentioned (above) are printed with Dummy (or placeholder) text. This text is the reading material viewed by the Fifth Man sitting in 1 of 2 stalls. [Sherlock Holmes Anthology].* 566 pages. Mankato: Liver Pizza Press. ISBN 9781365577390.

Van Buskirk, Todd (2017-01-04). *The Concert Register of Carlo Maria Giulini (1914-2005) is printed (starting on page 7) with every concert featuring the music of Anton Bruckner (1824-1896) printed in the color of red (the frontispiece on page 2 is a reference to this idea). The inspiration for printing the words of Jesus in red comes from Luke 22:20 - "This cup is the new testament in my blood, which I shed for you". On June 19, 1899, Louis Klopsch (1852-1910) conceived the idea while working on an editorial. Klopsch asked his mentor Rev. T. De Witt Talmage what he thought of a testament with the words spoken by Jesus printed in red ink and Dr. Talmage replied, "It could do no harm and it most certainly could do much good." [poems].* 150 pages. Mankato: Liver Pizza Press.

Van Buskirk, Todd, ed. (2017-01-18). *"'The Most Reverend'" (W. Laabs, personal communication, 2008, p.207) is a style applied primarily within the historic denominations of Christianity. In the Catholic Church Archbishops bear the style "The Most Reverend". "Street Evangelist" (p.207) is a combination of two meanings. The evangelist is one that travels from town to town spreading the gospel of Jesus Christ. Street preaching is the act of publicly proselytizing a religious message to crowds of people in open places and is usually associated with*

Evangelical Protestant Christianity (Dillon, 2008, personal communication, p.81). Originally, Ventriloquism (p.207) was a religious practice. The name comes from the Latin for to speak from the stomach, i.e. venter (belly) and loqui (speak). One of the earliest recorded group of prophets to utilize this technique was the Pythia, the priestess at the temple of Apollo in Delphi, who acted as the conduit for the Delphic Oracle. By the late 18th century, ventriloquist performances were an established form of entertainment in England. In the 1790s performers were beginning to incorporate dolls or a Puppet (p.207) into their performance, notably the Irishman James Burns who "... carries in his pocket, an ill-shaped doll, a broad face, which he exhibits ... as giving utterance to his own Childish Jargon [emphasis added]." [collected letters]. 222 pages. Mankato: Liver Pizza Press.

Van Buskirk, Todd (2017-01-21). *The 1st movement (Ruhig schreitend) of Anton Webern's Symphony Op.21 is a meditation on the first 13 bars (Andante Comodo) of Mahler's 9th (see fig.1 on page 209).*

Particularly the first 14 bars (see fig.2 on page 21) with it's "arrhythmic heartbeat" rhythm. Webern evokes the Mahler 9 while also structuring the notes into a "double four part canon in contrary motion" according to Rene Leibowitz, who also notes that the "instrumentation participates in the individualization of the various parts" of each canon. [symphony (no.2)]. 212 pages. Mankato: Liver Pizza Press. ISBN 9781365688584.

Veauvy, Rozenn (2014-11-02). *Miscellanées.* [14/28 blank pages]. Zürich: LUMA Foundation (1000 BOOKS BY 1000 POETS). ISBN 9781312648340.

Velasco, Efraín (2015). *Sostiene Gruñón.* Centro de cultura digital.

Velasco, Efraín (2016). *Poliedro, c.2011.* Tokonama Ed (Col. La Oficinista).

Vella, Cathy (2011-12-31). *Heights Wuthering.* 174 pages. Lulu.com. ISBN 9781471035548.

Venet, Bernar (1999). *Apoétiques: 1967-1998.* 144 pages. Genève: Musee d'Art Moderne et Contemporain. ISBN 9782940159123.

Ventura, Alejandro (2013-11-18). *SPECULATIVE 2014 WHITNEY BIENNIAL*

EXHIBITION CATALOGUE. 105 pages. TROLL THREAD.

Ventura, Alejandro (2014). *The Tempest*. 49 pages. Gauss PDF.

Victor, Divya (2011). *Punch*. [45 pages]. Gauss PDF.

VICTOR, DIVYA (2011-04-18). *PARTIAL DICTIONARY OF THE UNNAMABLE*. 52 pages. TROLL THREAD.

VICTOR, DIVYA (2011-10-31). *PARTIAL DIRECTORY OF THE UNNAMABLE*. 116 pages. TROLL THREAD.

Victor, Divya (2012). *Goodbye, John!*. [1017 pages]. Gauss PDF.

VICTOR, DIVYA (2012-11-05). *PARTIAL DERIVATIVE OF THE UNNAMABLE*. [40 pages]. TROLL THREAD.

Victor, Divya (2014). *SWIFT TAXIDERMIES 1919-1922*. [21 pages]. Gauss PDF.

Victor, Divya (2014-04-29). *Things To Do With Your Mouth*. 134 pages. Los Angeles: Les Figues Press. ISBN 9781934254523.

Vicuña, Cecilia (2002). *Instan*. 88 pages. Berkeley: Kelsey Street Press. ISBN 0932716504.

vidler, catherine (2016-09-16). *chaingrass*. 234 pages. SOd press. ISBN 9781326765392.

Viegener, Matias, and Wertheim, Christine, eds. (2007-09-00). *The /n/oulipian Analects*. 256 pages.

Los Angeles: Les Figues Press. ISBN 9781934254004.

Viegener, Matias (2012-10-01). *2500 Random Things About Me Too*. 255 pages. Los Angeles: Les Figues Press. ISBN 9781934254356.

Vilandt, Joakim (2014-03-01). *Larmens antologi*. [46 pages]. Zürich: LUMA Foundation (1000 BOOKS BY 1000 POETS). ISBN 9781304908834.

Vilgrain, Bénédicte (2002-06-00). *sku (Une grammaire tibétaine, chapitre deux)*. 28 pages. Bordeaux: Éditions de l'Attente. ISBN 9782914688062.

Villa, José Garcia (2008-07-29). *Doveglion: Collected Poems*; edited by John Edwin Cowen. 304 pages. New York: Penguin Books. ISBN 9781101662687.

Voragen, Roy (2016-04-12). *YOUR LIPS StUttER*. Gauss PDF.

Voragen, Roy (2016-06-00). *Primal #74207281*. 97 pages. SOd press.

Waldrop, Rosmarie (1970). *Camp Printing*. [24 pages]. Providence: Burning Deck.

Waldrop, Rosmarie (1981). *Nothing Has Changed*. 35 pages. Windsor: Awede Press.

Waldrop, Rosmarie (1986-11-28). *Streets Enough to Welcome Snow*. 80

pages. Barrytown: Station Hill Press, Inc.

Waldrop, Rosmarie (1987-11-01). *The Reproduction of Profiles*. 86 pages. New York: New Directions. ISBN 9780811210456.

Waldrop, Rosmarie (1988). *shorter american memory*. 28 pages. Providence: Paradigm Press. ISBN 9780945926054.

Walker, Nathan (2013-04-29). *The Invention of Collage Reduced to Material Objects*. 44 pages. Lulu.com.

Walker, Rob (2015-02-11). *Businessman Hands*. [3 pages + MP3]. Gauss PDF.

Walker, Wendy (2009). *Blue Fire*. 253 pages. New York: Proteotypes Books. ISBN 9780980000153.

Wagenknecht, Addie (2014-08-11). *Technological Selection of Fate*. 112 pages. Brescia: LINK Editions. ISBN 9781291936513.

Wandeler-Deck, Elisabeth (2009-04-00). *Da liegt noch ihr Schal*. 268 pages. Bern: edition taberna kritika. ISBN 9783905846065.

Wandeler-Deck, Elisabeth (2013-01-00). *Ein Fonduekoch geworden sein*. 84 pages. Bern: edition taberna kritika. ISBN 9783905846225.

Wandeler-Deck, Elisabeth (2015-10-00). *Das Heimweh der*

Meeresschildkröten. 262 pages. Bern: edition taberna kritika. ISBN 9783905846362.

Ward, Matthew George Richard (2010). *Picture 380*. [117 pages]. Gauss PDF.

Warhol, Andy (1968). *a, A Novel*. 451 pages. New York: Grove Press.

Warman, Laura A. (2015). *DRONE LOVE*. [48 double pages]. Gauss PDF.

Watier, Éric (2015-10-00). *Plus c'est facile, plus c'est beau: prolégomènes à la plus belle exposition du monde*. 96 pages. Rennes: éditions incertain sens. ISBN 9782914291712.

Way, Nyein (2013-01-28). *Uncreative Manifesto (2005)*. Calgary: No press.

Way, Nyein (2016-01-00). *Wittgenstein's Lab(1): Biopsy of Silence. uncorrected / unedited realities (1962-2063)*. Yangon: Kabanaryeegyi Publishing House.

Weichbrodt, Gregor (2014-02-06). *On the Road*. [70 pages]. Zürich: LUMA Foundation (1000 BOOKS BY 1000 POETS). ISBN 9781304882769.

Weichbrodt, Gregor (2015-01-10). *I Don't Know*. 357 pages. Berlin: Frohmann Verlag/0x0a. ISBN 9783944195605.

Weichbrodt, Gregor (2015-01-26). *Chicken Infinite*. 500 pages. 0x0a. ISBN 9781291879315.

Weichbrodt, Gregor (2015-12-13). *Gruntgesets*. 136 pages. 0x0a.

Weichbrodt, Gregor (2015-11-29). *BÆBEL*. 686 pages. 0x0a.

Weichbrodt, Gregor (2016-09-29). *Dictionary of non-notable Artists*. 129 pages. Berlin: Frohmann Verlag/0x0a. ISBN 9783944195421.

Weichbrodt, Gregor, and Bajohr, Hannes (2015-04-26). *Glaube Liebe Hoffnung: Nachrichten aus dem christlichen Abendland*. 80 pages. 0x0a. ISBN 9781326256968.

Weichbrodt, Gregor, and Bennett, Vicki (2015-01-26). *The Fundamental Questions*. 569 pages. 0x0a.

Weichbrodt, Gregor, and Stanjek, Grischa (2011). *Das ist der Tag, von dem ihr noch euern Enkelkindern erzählen werdet*. Berlin: Buchbinderei Christian Klünder.

Weichbrodt, Gregor, and Stanjek, Grischa (2013). *Die Revolution*. ISBN 9783518125533.

Weiner, Hannah (1982). *Code Poems [Poems for the Use of All Nations]*. [31 pages]. Barrytown: Open Studio. ISBN 0940170035.

Weiner, Hannah (1985). *WRITTEN IN/The Zero One*. 32 pages. Victoria: Post Neo Publications.

Weiner, Hannah (2006-11-15). *Hannah Weiner's Open House*. 178 pages. Chicago: Kenning Editions. ISBN 9780976736417.

Weiner, Hannah (2008). *WEEKS*. Photographs by Barbara Rosenthal. 88 pages. West Lima: Xexoxial Editions. ISBN 9780977004973. [First edition published in (1990).]

Weiss, Jason, ed. (2002-01-15). *Back in No Time: The Brion Gysin Reader*. xiv; 354 pages. Middletown: Wesleyan University Press. ISBN 9780819565297.

Welsh, Michael (2013-07-02). *Self Help*. 57 pages. Portland: Jank Editions / Publication Studio and Social Malpractice Publishing. ISBN 9781624620355.

Wershler-Henry, Darren (2000-04-01). *the tapeworm foundry: andor the dangerous prevalence of imagination*. Toronto: House of Anansi Press. ISBN 9780887846526.

Wertheim, Christine (2007-09-01). *+|'me'S-pace, doc. 001.b*. 112 pages. Los Angeles: Les Figues Press. ISBN 9780976637196.

Whittock, Nick (2016-08-17). *faulkner*. [16 pages]. SOd press.

Wilson, Daniel (2016-02-02). *Files I Have Known: Data Reminiscences.* [29 pages]. Gauss PDF.

Wilson IV, Wilmer (2016-09-05). *['', 'Skin', ',', 'White', 'Masks'].* [64 pages]. Gauss PDF Editions.

why, emily (2014-02-00). *nocturnal admissions.* [28 pages]. Gauss PDF.

Wilkes, James (2009-10-00). *Reviews.* 24 pages. London: Veer Books. ISBN 9781907088025.

Williams, Emmett (1973-06-00). *A Valentine For Noël.* [280 pages]. New York: Something Else Press. [The poem *SOLDIER* has been republished separately in 2015 by the publishing house Zédélé Éditions, Brest, ISBN 9782915859386.]

Wilner, Brandon (2015-09-03). *The Complete Works of Brandon Wilner.* Calgary: Spacecraft Press.

Wolf, Uljana (2009). *falsche freunde.* 87 pages. Idstein: kookbooks verlag. ISBN 9783937445380.

Wolgamot, John Barton (2001). *In Sara, Mencken, Christ and Beethoven There Were Men and Women.* Edited by Keith Waldrop and Robert Ashley. 116 pages. New York: Lovely Music. ISBN 0967997410. [First edition: 1944; self-published.]

Woodall, John (1977-05-00). *Recipe: collected thoughts for considering the void*. [20 pages]. Berkeley: Tuumba Press.

Worth, Liz (2015-09-00). *No Work Finished Here: Rewriting Andy Warhol*. 462 pages. Toronto: BookThug. ISBN 9781771661645.

Xisto, Pedro (1966). *a e i o u [ou Vogaláxia]*. [8 pages]. São Paulo: Invenção.

Yau, John (2002-03-26). *Borrowed Love Poems*. 133 pages. New York: Penguin Poets. ISBN 9780142000519.

Yearous-Algozin, Joseph (2010). *THE LAZARUS PROJECT: ALIEN VS. PREDATOR*. [20 pages]. TROLL THREAD.

Yearous-Algozin, Joey (2011). *The Lazarus Project: Friday the 13th*. [25 pages]. Gauss PDF.

Yearous-Algozin, Joseph (2011-07-28). *BURIED*. [36 pages]. TROLL THREAD.

Yearous-Algozin, Joey (2012-04-22). *9/11 911 CALLS IN 911 PT. FONT*. [2 volumes; 464/460 pages]. TROLL THREAD.

Yearous-Algozin, Joey (2012-06-22). *The Lazarus Project: Night and Fog*. [32 pages]. TROLL THREAD.

Yearous-Algozin, Joey (2012-10-10). *The Lazarus Project: Heaven*. [92 pages]. TROLL THREAD.

Yearous-Algozin, Joey (2012-12-03). *The Lazarus Project: Nine Eleven*. [132 pages]. TROLL THREAD.

Yearous-Algozin, Joey (2013-06-19). *The Lazarus Project: MyDeathSpace.com*. [3 volumes; 504 pages each]. TROLL THREAD.

YEAROUS-ALGOZIN, JOEY (2013-10-15). *REAL KILL LIST*. [14 pages]. TROLL THREAD.

YEAROUS-ALGOZIN, JOEY (2013-11-18). *ZERO DARK 30 PT. FONT*. [518 pages]. TROLL THREAD.

YEAROUS-ALGOZIN, JOEY (2014-05-09). *POETRY WALL STREET VISUAL POETRY*. TROLL THREAD.

YEAROUS_ALGOZIN, JOEY (2015-04-20). *DEMO BOOK FOR INTERN*. [674 pages]. TROLL THREAD.

Yearous-Algozin, Joey (2016-05-16). *CALLER REMOVED*. [156 pages]. TROLL THREAD.

Yearous-Algozin, Joey (2016-07-19). *how to stop worrying abt the state of publishing when the world's burning and everybody's broke anyways and all you really care abt is if anyone is even reading yr work*. [3 pages]. TROLL THREAD.

YEAROUS_ALGOZIN, JOEY (2016-10-11). *JJ'S KIDS*. [109 pages]. Gauss PDF.

Yoon, Hyung-Min (2012). *Backwards Metamorphosis Library: In 18 Volumes*. 1050 pages. Vancouver:

Publication   Studio.   ISBN 9781927385067.

Yvroud, Claude (2006-05-00). *D'une poésie saisissante*. 74 pages. Bordeaux: Éditions de l'Attente. ISBN 9782914688468.

Zajac, Ondřej (2011). *Kafegrafie*. Praha: Petr Štengl. ISBN 9788087563007.

Zambon, Ludivine (2014-02-25). *Texte*. [18/32 blank pages]. Zürich: LUMA Foundation (1000 BOOKS BY 1000 POETS). ISBN 9781312048737.

Zboya, Eric (2010-03-00). *Emily Dickinson's 'I lost a World – the other day!': An Algorithmic Translation*. Calgary: No press.

Zboya, Eric (2011). *UN COUP DE DÉS JAMAIS N'ABOLIRA LE HASARD. Translations in Higher Dimensions*. 98 pages. /ubu editions.

Zboya, Eric (2011-12-17). *THE NOBLE GASES*. Calgary: No press.

Zits, Paul (2013-03-20). *Massacre Street*. 128 pages. The University of Alberta Press. ISBN 9780888646750. [Excerpt previously published in (2010-09-00). Calgary: No press.]

Zolf, Rachel (2007-03-00). *Human Resources*. 96 pages. Toronto: Coach House Books. ISBN 9781552451823.

Zolf, Rachel (2010-02-22). *Neighbour Procedure*. 96 pages. Toronto: Coach House Books. ISBN 1552452298.

Zolf, Rachel (2014-10-07). *Janey's Arcadia*. 136 pages. Toronto: Coach House Books. ISBN 9781552452950.

Zultanski, Steven (2010-06-15). *PAD*. 165 pages. Los Angeles: Make Now Press. ISBN 9780981596235.

Zultanski, Steven (2010-11-01). *Cop Kisser*. 196 pages. Toronto: BookThug. ISBN 9781897388709.

Zultanski, Steven (2012-12-18). *Agony*. 158 pages. Toronto: BookThug. ISBN 9781927040409.

Zultanski, Steven (2014-12-01). *Bribery*. 112 pages. New York: Ugly Duckling Presse. ISBN 9781937027308.

ki 001
khora impex // 2017

www.ingramcontent.com/pod-product-compliance
Lightning Source LLC
Chambersburg PA
CBHW020424290526
45785CB00002B/714